Contents

Get Smart!
About Modern Career
Development

A Personal Guide to
Creating Your Life's Work

Michelle L. Casto

Get Smart! Publishing

Get Smart! About Modern Career Development
A Personal Guide to Creating Your Life's Work
Copyright August 2000, Michelle L. Casto

First Printing: October 2000

Library of Congress Number: 00-092181
ISBN Softcover: 0-96747404-5-5

Publisher: Get Smart! Publishing
           Atlanta, GA

Website: www.getsmartseries.com

Get Smart! LearningBooks are distributed by Ingram Book Company.

DEDICATION

This book is warmly dedicated to all of the men and women who wish to create their life's work. It is my hope that through the use of the Get Smart! decision-making process that you will raise your self awareness, practice active reflection, and trust your intuition—and as a result will achieve all of your career aspirations.

ACKNOWLEDGEMENTS

A book such as this comes from a lifetime
of learning opportunities through formal
and informal work experiences.
It is because of my keen interest in career development
that I am able to share these insights with you.

To Darlene Martin, for reading and commenting on the manuscript.

To Ann Kempner Fisher, for editing and supporting my writing.

To Scott Sherman, for creating the book cover and Get Smart! logo.

Thank You!

"The first duty of a human being is to assume the right relationship with society—more briefly, to find your real job and do it."

—Charlotte Perkins Gilman

From the Author...

"Whatever you can do, or dream you can, begin it.
Boldness has genius, power, and magic in it."
—Johann Von Goethe

How many times have you felt like you were meant to do something special, but just couldn't figure out what is was? You, along with a million others have experienced the human emotion of frustration from having unique gifts and talents to share, but no place to display them. You have also probably worked in ill-fitting environments and ended up feeling disillusioned and frustrated. Like you, I have felt this way, but finally, I came to view each of my work experiences as learning opportunities. And I made a conscious decision to take away what I needed to learn from each job. I have put my experiences and knowledge to work in the form of *Get Smart! About Modern Career Development: A Personal Guide to Creating Your Life's Work.* I know that *you* have the capacity to make smarter career decisions. You just need to learn how!

My life purpose is to educate and empower people to make smarter decisions in important life areas, which is how the *Get Smart!* idea evolved from a random thought to a workshop, to an interactive LearningBook. Unlike other self-help career books, you will not find a "magic pill" that holds all the answers to your questions. In fact, after reading and working through this book, you may have more questions than ever, which believe it or not, will help your decision-making skills. Because as the saying goes, *"The one who questions never loses his way."*

The *Get Smart!* approach to modern career development is individually designed and defined by you. With the help of *Get Smart!* you will decide for yourself what you need from your life's work. Self-awareness, active reflection, and intuitive guidance are the key components of **smart** decision-making. This book has been designed to be a self-discovery tool. It includes numerous activities and journal assignments to help you learn about yourself. By deciding today that you want to *Get Smart!* you have decided to live in awareness and become empowered to make choices that will bring you the most fulfillment.

Because I have learned to listen to my head as well as my heart, I have made smarter career choices. Through my research, I have learned that there are thousands of creative and competent people out there with so much to offer, but who cannot seem to find meaning in their work. They too, made the not-so-smart decision of working in unhealthy work environments, only to end up unhappy and unfulfilled. This is because they chose to buy into outdated career myths instead of choosing to live in awareness of the current reality. It is my belief that this mistake and the misery it creates can be avoided by simply applying a smarter approach to your career development process.

Because our careers often are not sought out, researched, or even given much conscious thought, people tend to "fall into jobs" based on little self-awareness. And then we begin to feel stuck and soon become unable or unwilling to make a career change.

The current labor statistics say that on average, people will change career fields (not just jobs) an average of 5-7 times in a lifetime. Thus, it is imperative that we learn how to find new ways to apply our skills in a changing marketplace. Indeed, you need to become better informed on what is out there in the career market. You also need to become an active participant in creating your life's work by utilizing an effective decision-making process.

One of the work myths of today is that there is security in staying the same. The truth is, in the modern working world, you need to stretch and bend, to shape and reshape yourself to the changing needs of society. We cannot afford to stay the same, to do things the same way. We are entering a new world order—and we must adapt or become extinct.

Everyone needs to feel that they are contributing. And we often seek meaning from our work, but we also need to realize that work is just one way we can express our inner self. As living, breathing, thinking, and feeling human beings, we also need oxygen, food, water, exercise, intellectual and emotional stimulation, friendship, fun, romance, and much more to live a fulfilled life. It's vital to strive for balance in all of these areas.

Smart people know that before you can create your life's work, you must first undergo a thorough self assessment. This book will help you to do some intense soul searching, which is necessary to prepare you for a meaningful career. In fact, the first half of the book is focused on how to become prepared for your work.

Being proactive enables you to move along your career path naturally because you are intentional and mindful of the direction in which you are headed. Living by your vision enables you to work with purpose because when you *"follow your bliss,"* as Joseph Campbell once suggested, opportunities present themselves in unexpected ways. Living in awareness will help you make decisions on a more intuitive level, a level that will guide you to your life purpose.

How can you uncover the work that you are meant to do? By developing "inner guidance," a road map if you will. Intuition is the internal faculty that humans possess that provides direction. Intuition will lead you to the kind of career you desire and deserve. But this requires a strong belief that you possess a higher self that knows what is best for you.

How do you develop your intuition? Your first step will be to use this book to learn about yourself. In order to see results, I ask that you read this book with a willingness to *Get Smart!* and a desire to make positive changes. The journal assignments are a journey to your inner knowing. Success requires that you set aside your personal beliefs and begin to perceive your career on a more realistic and intuitive level. I believe that after reading and working with this book, you will begin to see an increase in positive and uplifting events. This will be a direct result of your ability to *Get Smart!* by allowing you're your higher, more intuitive self to make your choices, and increase your chances of creating the career of your dreams.

Michelle L. Casto
August 2000

How To Use This Book

"We cannot become what we want by remaining what we are."
—Max Dupree

Dear Reader:

This is not your typical self-help book. You will not come away with *the answer* about your career. As you have already figured out, there are no easy answers to some of life's tougher questions, such as "How do I create my life's work?" However, I can assure you that you will have quite a few revelations about yourself. What you do with the information is entirely up to you!

  Get Smart! About Modern Career Development is not about how to get a job. There are plenty of books on the market if you want just some form of employment. *Get Smart!* is about how to create a lifetime of fulfillment—a career that incorporates your need to actively contribute to improving the world by utilizing your unique talents, skills, and abilities. It is your personal guide to uncovering your unique gifts and deciding where and how you will use them.

  Unlike other career development books, you will not find one perfect formula for success, but rather a philosophy of what the meaning of your work life is. By raising your self-awareness, practicing active reflection, and developing intuitive guidance, you will learn how to consciously create the kind of life you have always wanted. You will learn the process of career development which is a skill you will use throughout your lifetime, no matter what stage of your life you may be in.

  David McCullough once said, *"Real success is finding your life's work in the work that you love."* Finding *your* life's work is about creating a lifestyle. In this book, you will explore important questions such as, *What would I do even if I didn't get paid for it? What do I feel my life purpose is? How do I need to express my inner self to the world? What is the "it" that I must do?*

I also encourage you to use this LearningBook as a resource that you can refer to again and again. Using this book in conjunction with your own journal will empower you to make thoughtful, smart decisions. Reading, reflecting, and writing will provide the framework for those decisions that will lead to positive changes in your career. *Get Smart!* means becoming aware of how you *think and feel* about work in order to turn around your not-so-smart work habits. You will learn about the modern world of work, and the choices that come with it, which will energize your career because you will realize that you can do work that is meaningful to you.

My ultimate wish is that you will gain a new and enlightened perspective about what you are seeking from your working life. And in so doing, will accomplish your wildest dreams. As a result, I hope you will become inspired to share what you learn with a friend or colleague. To be an effective learner about your career, you will need the following:

1) An open mind and heart
2) A desire to consciously create a more meaningful life
3) A readiness to make some significant life changes
4) A favorite pen and journal

Let's get you started on the path to creating your life's work...

Chapter One

Get Smart!
Decision-Making

"There is an art of which everyone should be a master—
the art of reflection.
If you are not a thinking human,
to what are you human at all."
—Samuel Coleridge

Get Smart!

Of course you want to make more educated and enlightened decisions relating to your career development or you wouldn't be reading this book. And truly, the best way to energize your career is to change your attitude and the way you think about work. The Get Smart! decision-making approach to career development includes raising your self-awareness, utilizing active reflection, listening to your intuitive guidance, and then making an educated decision. Throughout this book, you will be raising your self-awareness. It is important to know that if at any time, you feel lost or confused, that you go back to the initial step of understanding yourself because the person who truly knows him or herself is the person most capable of making smart decisions.

We've all heard of people who use "half a brain" when making decisions or those who make a half-hearted attempt at their work. *Get Smart!* reminds us that we need to use our whole brain and whole heart when making important decisions. The fact that we were given these special gifts is proof enough that we have the capability of getting smarter about our own career development.

In the modern world, there are many different professional

opportunities available to us. More than any other time in history, we have more diverse people performing different kinds of work than ever before. Because not everyone wants or needs the same things from work, it is imperative that we pre-determine what we are looking for from our professional lives, lest we fall into one unfulfilling position after another. Today's workplace is constantly changing to keep up with the changes in our society, and there are many different ways to work, not all of which may be right for you. So, instead of trying to fit into a square peg, discover your unique shape of work. Believe in the spirit of you!

People who are happy in their jobs seem to have found the perfect fit between their talents, training, interests, and values. The environment they have placed themselves in allows them to express who they really are. In return, the person gives to their work 110% because of the inherent satisfaction. It is that sense of "perfect fit" that all of us are seeking.

As human beings, we want to feel we are valued and needed. And we want to be appreciated and recognized for our talents and skills. To *Get Smart!* is to raise your consciousness, and in so doing, change your perceptions of life and work. It is also about learning from your past jobs and positions. It is important to avoid choosing the wrong kind of job, because when we are in the wrong work environment, we learn the wrong way to work, waste precious time and energy, and become disillusioned. Often, we get off track in our careers, due to our internal conflict of doing what we "should" do (based on society's standards) instead of doing what we want do, according to our inner nature. It is this disconnect between our human experience and our Spirit that causes career confusion. People forget who they really are and why they are here, and they end up doing something ill-suited to them.

In life, we struggle with our inner knowing and outer information. We usually make decisions based on the outer information, rather than intuition. When this happens, we usually get what we think we want from life, instead of getting what we need. Oftentimes, what we think we want to do with our life is not what *we need to do.* Our Spirit sees what is right for us and knows that we are meant to do something else. If we could only learn to follow our deepest intuition, we would end up with everything we need and want— including the right job, the right person, the right life. We just have to be open to what comes to us wrapped in a different package than what we expected!

Our ultimate work is to make our world a better place in which to live and love. Our life's work is what we want to share and provide to others while we are here on earth. When we live our purpose, we create it with conscious intention and smart decisions. Work offers us the opportunity to create life as we would like it. What we as a society focus on—what work we perform—reflects what we believe is important. As the needs of society evolve, new work is created that must be done. Work serves as a major vehicle for our evolution—we must be conscious of the work that we do and how we do it. Kahlil Gibran wrote, *"Work is love made visible."* In whatever we do, we express our love, therefore if we can find our right work, we can express even more love. Modern work needs the human touch of love.

There has long been a prevailing attitude that "work sucks," and is frequently equated with punishment. In Matthew Fox's book, *The Reinvention of Work*, he explains how work is often related to sin, or punishment for sinning, instead of its true meaning: an expression of our Godliness. Only when we are in touch with our spiritual self can we truly live up to our full potential. If more people lived up to their potential and were doing the were they were meant to do, our world could more quickly evolve.

"Be careful what you wish for, it just might come true" are wise words of caution. Often, our concept of our ideal "work" is different that the reality. Suppose, after reading this book, you decide that you want to become an artist. On the positive side is the use of creativity and freedom of expression, but the negative side is living on little or no income for a long time. We often don't want to think about the sacrifices that we have to make in order to fulfill our dreams, but there are always some. We don't realize the "down side" to certain types of work until we actually do it. However, using *Get Smart!* will empower you to learn ahead of time what you are getting yourself into!

Practice Active Reflection

The process of preparing yourself for work and choosing a career path is complex and often confusing. In order to make well thought-out, smart decisions, it is helpful to engage in active reflection. To be *active* means to focus energy towards an activity, and to *reflect* is "to ponder/meditate." *Active reflection* is to invest energy toward your thought process, which will enable you to tap into your intuition. It is consciously thinking about what you do before you actually do it. Through active reflection, a process central to the *Get Smart!* approach, you can more accurately interpret what is going on in your work, which will lead to smarter career choices.

As is true with all processes, when new information becomes available, perspectives change. As your own life purpose unfolds, revealing more of what you may not have been aware of, your thoughts and feelings alter or change completely. Unfortunately, our thought processes can be much like a computer that shuts down. Most of us unconsciously choose to disregard relevant information, particularly about our careers—it's as if *we* "shut down." We become unable to process new information and/or move forward. What needs to happen is when new data becomes available, we immediately make a mental note and then check it out against what we already know. This allows us to analyze our thoughts and feelings.

We lose our ability to comprehend anything contrary to what we *want to believe.* Foolishly, we make up our minds about a job field or industry with little or no real information. When we are unable or unwilling to process new information, it is usually because we do not like to admit that we made a bad choice. In order to compensate for this, we convince ourselves that we are still right even though we know, somewhere deep down, that we are really wrong. When we are not able to clearly perceive, hear, and understand what is going on, we tend to make not-so-smart decisions.

Active reflection includes the elements of understanding yourself, gathering information about the world of work, making sense of how this "fits you" and finally deciding what to do about it. In order for it to be effective, it requires that you be completely honest with yourself about your strengths, weaknesses, interests and skills. By "actively" engaging in deep thought (reflection) through talking about it with a trusted friend or writing about it in your journal, you are "working" with the information, thus internalizing it.

An example of lack of reflection is when you take classes and sit through a lecture, but never actively listen, write down, or talk about the material presented. When this happens, you rarely retain the information. You do not gain knowledge and you do not learn. Likewise, if you take a passive approach to your life's work, you will not learn important lessons. On the other hand, if you choose to actively engage yourself in your career decisions, you "get smart" and are able to make the necessary changes. Change is a central component to personal growth and development. Change is the very essence of life, especially in the modern world, and a willingness to change is essential to creating your true life's work.

Once you begin to use active reflection, you will begin to see your career path more clearly. When you have mastered active reflection, it will be easy to know what kind of work will most fulfill you and make you the happiest.

Follow Your Intuitive Guidance

Florence Scovel, a theologian, once said, *"Intuition is the spiritual faculty that doesn't explain; it seemingly points the way."* It's also been said that intuition is your divine Spirit talking to you. If we stop for a moment and acknowledge this, we realize the incredible perspective we have. Unfortunately, this is a perspective we often choose to ignore because it is an undeveloped skill. Using your intuition when making important decisions allows you to move along your path easily and effortlessly. You don't have to struggle and worry, because things fall naturally into place when you follow your inner nature. Developing your intuitive guidance (your inner voice) is essential to smart decision- making and career choices, and includes balancing your cognitive (thinking) abilities with your affective (feeling) abilities.

Synthesize information from your head and your heart, and bring them into your consciousness. You only have to learn how to develop these powers and I promise that it will become second nature to you. The first step is obviously to become aware that *you* contain this amazing power. But you must consciously choose to use it!

Next, you have to realize that when dealing with matters of work, there can be some discrepancies between what the mind thinks and what the heart feels. When we *think* about work, we focus on what we should do so that we can pay the bills, etc., which only takes into account the practical side. When we *feel* about work, we focus on what we want to do and consider the impractical, such as moving to a foreign country. We very rarely take the time to see how the two sides can meet and form a whole new possibility. When making a major life decision, such as *"What should I do as my life's work?"* it is pretty safe to say that our equilibrium is all out of whack. And we tend to do one of two things: We either throw out all rational behavior altogether or block any and all emotions from our consciousness. We need to learn to align these two extremes, balance them, and make decisions from a true state of *knowing*, which is our intuition. You can learn to take these two seemingly opposing faculties and fuse them to have single-ness of purpose and direction.

The best way to do this is to be clear on what you are looking for from your career, so that you can then allow your intuitive nature to take over. The key is to believe that your higher self sees what is best for you. Indeed, Spirit is trying to send you messages, but you must learn to open up and receive the information in order for it to make a difference in your life. Once you have learned to have faith in this process, your heart and mind will function together for greater harmony than you ever dreamed possible.

By following your intuition, you become empowered. When you are empowered, you trust that you know the right thing to do—despite what other people might say. You look within yourself for direction.

Dis-empowered people look for answers outside of themselves. They turn to others to find the answers to their life, and thus become confused and often misguided. Confused people are easy to spot—they tend to change their minds almost on a daily basis. It stands to reason that if you are dis-empowered and confused, you will not be making decisions with clarity and focus.

If you are like most people, you prefer one faculty (thinking or feeling) over the other. People tend to use the one they are most comfortable with, but sometimes it is necessary to look at the situation through your "weaker" one.

You are **Head Strong** if you typically:
- Over-analyze people, things, and situations
- Consider the practical side of the issue
- Rationalize your behavior to yourself and to others
- Consider yourself first in situations
- Prefer thinking over feeling
- Ignore feelings contrary to your thinking when making decisions
- Hide your emotions
- Like to plan ahead
- Like to be in control
- Use the word NO a lot

You are **Heart Strong** if you typically:
- Are sensitive and emotional
- Consider the impractical side of the issue
- Feel things in the pit of your stomach
- Consider others first in situations
- Prefer feeling over thinking
- Ignore thoughts contrary to your feelings when making decisions
- Show your emotions
- Like to go with the flow
- Like to make others feel good
- Use the word YES a lot

Note: These represent extremes—there is no good or bad way to process information. But we do need bring these two into balance in order to make better decisions.

Both are ways of "sensing," but in order to be a more effective decision-maker, you need to use them in conjunction. On occasion, it may be more appropriate to listen with your heart, as it will provide the direction that you need to go. Other times, you may find that tapping into your head can save you from making "miss-takes" in your career. The key is to pick up on coincidences, signs, and other external messages by filtering them through both faculties to get the most accurate "reading." The real secret to intuitive guidance is to let your inner soul be your guide.

A "hunch" is accurate information from a higher intelligence, therefore, you can rely on it. You can further develop your intuitive guidance by preparing yourself by gathering the necessary information and experiences to provide more of an opportunity for your intuition to surface. Intuition cannot be forced, you need to allow it. After loading up your mind with information about the issue, give your intuition time to work on it. And then become open to the answer. You will likely experience an "Aha" moment, which is a moment of instant awareness, where the answer sprouts from "out of the blue."

Each person has a unique way of uncovering their intuition. Some people experience intuition as a feeling, others a gut reaction, others will see images or have a dream, others hear an actual message. Become familiar with how your inner self communicates with you. Once you receive the message, check it out with your research and common sense.

Smart Tip:

➡ If you are not 100% sure about something going on in your career (or life), stop and think before making a decision. Usually this is your intuition trying to tell you that something is not quite right.

Get Smart!

➡ Until head and heart are working in unison, you will continue to feel unfulfilled with your work.

Journal Assignment #1

Write about how well-developed your intuition is. What things can you do to enhance your intuitive nature? Think about starting small. Learn to listen to yourself. For example, you can begin by using your intuition to choose the quickest grocery line. Or by choosing to say "no" to a work project that doesn't feel right. As you begin to trust yourself, move on to more important decisions.

Go on a Treasure Hunt

How many times have you thought to yourself: I want to make a career change, but I can't because…? There are many ways to create *meaning* in your career, from changing your path entirely, changing environments, or changing how you feel about the work that you do. The question is how and when do you make these career changes? A better question may be "why." *Why make changes?* Usually it is because your inner voice is whispering to you that it is time to move on, to grow, and to change—a soulful yearning arises, and it is hard to ignore.

Before you do anything, it is important to stop and reflect on what you are looking for from a career. Are you looking for something more in the job you currently hold? Are you looking for a change in environment within the same field? Or are you looking to uncover a totally new career? If you are seeking meaning from your work, you are no doubt seeking something that is missing—perhaps your soul needs to express something to the world. Intuitive career guidance will tell you when to stay and when to move on to new roles, positions, experiences.

Planning a career can be likened to hunting for treasure. A metaphor that I often use when talking about job seekers is that of the "treasure hunter." There are three: the digger, the jumper, the intuitive.

The *digger* is the kind who picks a spot and digs and digs. Because they are so focused on the perceived value of the gold, they hardly take notice of how boring their work has become. They may not find gold or treasure, and often do not know when to stop digging. The *jumper* jumps around from spot to spot, panning on the surface, never venturing deeper to see what may be found below. Sometimes they may find a nugget, but most of the time, they miss the jackpot. The *intuitive* hunter uses intuition to lead them to the riches. They use a variety of approaches, depending on what their inner guidance tells them. They may sometimes dig deeper, try another location, or even change directions by ditching their pan in favor of a mine. This person often hits the jackpot!

In terms of your own career development, consider whether you choose a job or position and dig in deep, hoping to one day find some meaning. Or do you jump from job to job, position to position, company to company hoping to finally feel fulfilled. How about planning your career in accordance with your inner guidance, the small voice that tells you when to stay, when to go, and when to try something completely different?

Most people who have trouble following their intuition lack clarity of thought and purpose. Clearly, you must know what you are looking for and why you are looking. In order to create meaning in your career, you must discern the difference between a golden nugget of opportunity and something that is nothing more than "fool's gold."

What is you inner voice telling you—does it say to stay where you are? Or seek out another environment, reinvent yourself and find the meaning? Or explore another vocation altogether? You can learn to tap into your intuition by asking yourself the following questions that will help you uncover your direction:

What do I want to create or contribute to the world?
What is the "it" that I must do? (Paint it, draw it, build it, share it, teach it, promote it, develop it, manage it, write it, say it, etc).
What fills me with happiness at the thought of doing it?
What is important to me?

What is my unique purpose in life and how can I go about achieving it?
What would I do even if no one paid me for it?
What do I do that makes time go by effortlessly?
What kind of lifestyle do I desire?
What are my natural talents, skills, and abilities?
What motivates and inspires me?
What am I meant to do next?

Sometimes the last question is key. Creating our life's work will not happen overnight. In the meantime, we have to figure out what to do *next*. We have to be "in the moment" and on the path that we are on. Sometimes more meaning can be found by staying put and reinvesting in your commitment to your present job. Sometimes more meaning can be found by changing environments and re-inspiring yourself about your career. And for those who feel they have missed their mark entirely, more meaning can be found by undergoing a complete career overhaul, and re-engineering yourself for a new career field. Only you know what the right move is. The question is *"What are you going to do about it?"*

Each of these career transitions require courage. Courage is the ability to face difficulty or danger without letting fear stand in your way. Courage requires listening to yourself and believing there is a higher power that sees what is best for you. And then acting on what you know needs to be done. *Get Smart!* by becoming a courageous, intuitive treasure hunter. You can create meaning in your career and discover the professional riches that were waiting for you all along!

Become a Get Smart! Decision-Maker

The process of deciding on a career path can be complex and confusing. In order to make a "smart" decision, it is helpful to go through the process with "active reflection," meaning that you cognitively think about all of the relevant information at hand, as well as adapt and change as new information becomes available. And always be self-aware and listen to your intuition, which will make you *feel* informed and certain. *Keep in mind that you will go through this process throughout your lifetime.*

GET SMART!
Decision-Making Process:

Decide
Prepare
Explore
Compare
Self-Awareness/World of Work Information

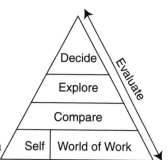

Step One—SELF ASSESSMENT
Know who you really are
(What are your strengths, weaknesses, and values?)
Identify all aspects of the self that relate to career decisions
➡ This step involves a thorough self investigation of your beliefs, interests, values, feelings, abilities, needs, ambitions, successes, lifestyle, etc. as well as your own level of self awareness and decision-making capability.

Career/occupational interests
Personal Style
Transferable skills
Motivation
Attitude
Aptitude
Values

Possible Questions: What kind of personality do I have? What are my special talents, interests, abilities? What are my values and how do they match available work environments?

Step Two—WORLD OF WORK INVESTIGATION
Determine the kind of work you want to do (What positions/roles match your strengths, weaknesses, and values?)
Research the world of work by field researching, networking, and informational interviewing
➡ This step involves a thorough investigation of the world of work and understanding how occupations are organized. For example: business, education, non-profit, technology, health care, information management, etc.

Occupations
Roles
Industry
Location
Product or Service
Compensation/Benefits Package
Growth Potential
Possible Questions: What careers exist today that will meet my employment needs? Are there positions that I can create that will meet my employment needs? In what careers could I envision myself being fulfilled?

Step Three—SYNTHESIS
Compare your personal style and interests with professional opportunities (Is there a potential match?)
Ask yourself what is the best fit given your current values, interests, skills, management style, career goals?
➡ This step involves the synthesizing of all of the information about yourself and the world of work to see if there is a potential fit.
Work is compatible with my personality
Matches my interests, skills, knowledge
Is consistent with my personal style
Intrinsically satisfying
Recognizing a match or mis-match
Possible Questions: How does this information seem to "mesh?" What career field would complement me? Which ones can be ruled out? Could I be successful doing_____?

Step Four—ROLE EXPLORATION
Explore your options ("Try-on" a few different short-term experiences before committing to a long-term assignment.)
What can you do to "try on" different jobs and roles?
➡ This step involves developing an exploration plan, where you can experience different jobs firsthand.
Temping
Internship or Cooperative Education
Informational Interviewing
Job Shadowing

Part-time work

Trying on different roles before making a final decision

Possible Questions: What can I do on a short-term basis to gain more exposure to these careers? Who can I talk to that could give me some information? What else do I need to do to gain entrance into these careers?

Step Five—PREPARATION

Prepare (Gain needed education or experience.)

What do you need to become prepared for entrance into your chosen profession?

➡ This step involves preparing for your career field by gaining the necessary qualifications.

Going back to school

Gaining credentials and experience

Talking to people in the industry

Developing a network by joining professional associations, etc

Taking the time necessary to "get prepared"

Possible Questions: How can I gain practical experience and additional knowledge? What job can I do in the meantime to help me break into my chosen career field? What organizations or people should I connect with?

Step Six—COMMITMENT

Make a decision (Based on where you are in life right now.)

Write a career strategy plan. Include your life vision, life purpose and "SMART" (Specific, Measureable, Achieveable, Reality-based, Time-limited) short-term/medium-term/long-term goals.

➡ This step involves making an educated decision and committing to the conscious pursuit of your career.

Developing your life vision and life purpose statements

Determining short-term goals and objectives

Making an action plan to achieve the goals

Setting a timeline for yourself

Identifying who may need to be involved to support you in your decision

Committing to your decision.

Possible Questions: What criteria will I use to make this decision? Who can help me make this decision? What can I do to become committed to this decision?

Be sure to *evaluate* your decision at each stage, so as to gather the best information. If you get lost along the way, always go back to step one—know yourself. The stages of the decision-making process are knowing that you need to make a decision, making the decision, and evaluating the decision. Career development is a lifelong process. As you change, your career goals and aspirations will also change. You will go through this process continually as you progress through the various stages of your life.

Place an "X" where you fall on each of these steps:

SELF-AWARENESS
How well do you know yourself?
Not all All_____Very Well

WORLD OF WORK KNOWLEDGE
How aware are you of your career options in the world of work?
Unaware_____Very Aware

POTENTIAL MATCH
How does this information seem to match up?
Not a Match_____Great Match

EXPLORATION
How willing are you to explore your options?
Not Willing to Explore_____Willing To Explore

PREPARATION
How prepared are you to move forward with your career choice?
Not Prepared_____Very Prepared

COMMITMENT
How willing are you to do what it takes to pursue this career choice?
Not Committed_____Very Committed

Learn what kind of decision-maker you are and strive to base your career decisions on your intuition (a balance of head and heart). For instance, if you typically make logical decisions, consider the creative aspects your situation presents. Throughout the decision-making process, you need to monitor your self-talk (what you say to yourself). Keep the messages positive: "I have the necessary information to make a decision." "I am confident that I will make the right decision." "I am a smart decision-maker." Reinvent ways to succeed. Turn a *limiting belief* into a belief that you can make the best decision. Change *lack of support* to finding new sources of support. Alter *lack of knowledge or experience* by gaining training and experience in your desired career field. Afterwards, analyze how things have changed, how you feel, and if there is more to be done.

Journal Assignment #2
Ask yourself: Where am I in the decision-making process? Has anything changed for me recently? What is stopping me from moving forward? What information do I need to gather to make a smart career decision?

Chapter Two

Raise Your Awareness

"To learn how to think is to learn how to live.
We, by our thinking, can bring
into our experiences whatever we desire, if we think correctly."
—Ernest Holmes

Self-awareness is the most important step towards smart decision-making. If you don't know yourself and what you are looking for, how can you possibly make a smart career decision? Know that self-awareness is a process. What you know about yourself today may be very different from tomorrow, next month, or ten years from now. The important thing is to learn to pay attention to what works for you and what doesn't, no matter where you are at in your life. Let's take a look at your current level of knowledge relating to work. If you consider yourself "clueless," congratulations! So are most people who are reading this book! Look at this as your opportunity to learn how to "get smarter."

Where Are You Now? Career Cluelessness or Career Confidence?
To find out, answer each of the following statements either True or False.

<u>Self Assessment</u>
1. If you are unclear about what your life's work should be, a qualified career counselor or career coach can you help you decide.
2. A career assessment is a tool to give you possible career options.
3. Being aware of your talents, knowledge, and skills is an important step in self-awareness.

4. Self-awareness is the first step in the Get Smart! decision-making process.

Self-Marketing Tools

5. Your resume should include your salary history.
6. You should put personal information like height, weight, and marital status on your resume.
7. A resume is always substituted for an application.
8. Your cover letter should be tailored to the position you are applying for.
9. You should dress professionally for your interview.
10. You can hand write a thank-you note.

Interview Finesse

11. The person who gets hired is always the one most qualified for the job.
12. Researching the company or position is part of the interview preparation process.
13. You should offer a firm handshake when you meet your interviewer.
14. It is wise to bring a typed list of references with you to the interview.
15. Be prepared to ask intelligent questions about the company during your interview.
16. When answering the "tell me about yourself" question, you should offer a two-minute summary of your resume.
17. "Mock interviews" are an excellent way to practice your interview skills.
18. One of your objectives during the interview is to find out if the position/company would be a good fit with your career aspirations.

Career Change

19. You will more than likely change careers more than once in the course of your life.
20. One way to continually find work is to keep your skills up-to-date.
21. Another way to continually find work is to develop and maintain a network.
22. Technology is a useful tool in the career search process.

Answers:

1-4:   True

5:       False (Salary information, if requested,
         goes into the cover letter).

6:       False (Leave off all personal information).

7:       False (If they request an application, you need to fill that out
         in addition to providing a resume).

8-10:   True

11:      False (The person who gets the job offer
         is often the one who interviews the best).

12-18:   True

19-22:   True

Get Smart!

➡ If you answered 18 or more correct: career confidence.

　　　14-17: career semi-cluelessness

　　　13 or less: career cluelessness

The Top Ten Not-So-Smart Things We Do in Work

1). Depend on the company or other people to take care of us.

2). Accept positions we really don't want.

3). Lie, cheat and steal to get ahead.

4). Sacrifice our personal life for our professional one.

5). Accept unethical language, thoughts and behavior
    as "the way it is in business."

6.) Learn unhealthy work behaviors from peers and supervisors.

7.) Work for people or corporations that are in direct
    conflict with our personal values.

8.) Refuse to stand up for what is right for fear of
    losing something (job, status, title).

9.) Lie or pretend about who we really are.

10.) Deny that there is a current work crisis in America.

Career Myths

There is one perfect career for me.

Just like there are no perfect people or places, there is no "perfect" career or company. The trick is to find a position that fits you best and displays your best self. A job is like a suit you wear; there are many you could try on and choose to wear, but you wouldn't wear the same one for your entire life! The same is true with a career. You will change outfits many times over, sometimes opting for outfits not in your normal wardrobe. Be open to the possibilities!

The reality is that there is no one job or position that is going to have everything or be "perfect." The key is to try to create the best life you can and to perform the best work you can.

The grass is greener somewhere other than here.

Job jumpers suffer from a low-grade depression because they mistakenly believe that the grass is going to be greener in another position or place. Every job, every corporation, every field of work has positive and negative points. You will not be any more satisfied anywhere else until you become empowered to make smart career (and life) decisions, which will always put you in your "right place."

If you have not found inner happiness, the reality is that no matter where you are, things will look better somewhere else. You have to learn to accept the good with the bad from your choice of vocation.

After I get a degree in _____, I will be done with my education and well prepared for my career.

The truth is that most degrees are obsolete within five years of completion. In order to stay marketable, you will have to become a *lifelong learner*, continually learning new things and adding to your repertoire of skills. Despite what some colleges may promise, there are no guarantees that a degree or certificate of any kind will prepare you for the real world of work. Things are changing so quickly, particularly in technological fields, that information quickly becomes outdated. The best any school can do is to teach you how to learn, how to take risks, how to develop team spirit, and how to be an honorable citizen.

The reality is that you need to learn how to learn and how to put your skills and talents to use continuously throughout your lifetime.

I will be happy when I find the "right" job.

It is true that finding the right kind of work can make you happier, but it cannot make you happy. Happiness is kind of an elusive feeling, and many people make the mistake of trying to find it in new jobs or with different partners. True happiness comes from within and is there even if you are in the "wrong" job. You have to make up your mind to be happy, so that when your career is a little off track, your whole world does not go to pieces. The truth is that there is no single "right" job, but many roles and positions that will enable you to share your talents and skills with others. It is not so much the kind of work you do, but the way you do your work that will bring you the most satisfaction.

The reality is that happiness comes from having balance in your life by receiving satisfaction in all areas, including labor, love, leisure, and learning.

The best jobs are found in the Fortune 500 companies.

Although there are many wonderful jobs in big corporations, most of the growth in the new world of work will be in small to medium companies, as well as those who choose to go into business for themselves. A similar myth is that a company will take care of you. Today, there is little loyalty—on either side—from employers or employees. The truth is that you will find yourself doing more short-term, contract work and relying on yourself, rather than on anyone else or any organization.

The reality is that you have a choice over the work that you do. A position at a Fortune 500 company is just one option out of a thousand that you could choose.

If I plan everything just right, I will have job security.

Planning, to some degree, is out the window. Because change is happening at an accelerated rate these days, the best laid plans can go awry. In the new world of work, planning is essential, but the best way to ensure your financial and emotional security is to become a career strategist—one who develops a multi-dimensional plan which is flexible and fluid. The other key is to become an active self-promoter—someone that can seek out and find people who need your talents and services.

The reality is that job searching/life planning is a lifelong endeavor. You will never be finished. You will begin to feel secure when you recognize that only you have power over what direction your career and life will take.

Know Your Work "Rights"

This activity is most effective when read aloud.

Right One
I have the right to enjoy my work.
Right Two
I have the right to a healthy and productive work environment.
Right Three
I have the right to be treated with care, respect and dignity
in all matters relating to my career and position.
Right Four
I have the right to be recognized for a job well done.
Right Five
I have the right to express myself through my work.
Right Six
I have the right to fair and reasonable compensation.
Right Seven
I have the right to a work environment that is safe.
Right Eight
I have the right to be treated equally and uniquely by others.
Right Nine
I have the right to surround myself with positive, productive,
and supportive co-workers.
Right Ten
I have the right to change career direction, if necessary, in order
to fulfill my life goals and aspirations.

Journal Assignment #3
Do you believe in any myths about work? Which ones? Have you ever
had your work rights violated? If so, how did you feel and what did you
do about it?

Chapter Three

Re-Program Yourself

"The way we choose to see the world creates the world we see."
—Barry Neil Kaufman

Eliminate Your Limiting Beliefs

Are you the kind of person who says to yourself: "I will never find the right career," or "I will always get stuck in dead-end jobs?" These types of statements are limiting beliefs; they are your psychological traffic lights—usually set to yellow for caution or red for stop. Since language plays a major role in how we define ourselves, the way we say things has an impact on what we will be able to do. For instance, if you use words like "can't," "never," or "always" and you believe the words to be true, you will not achieve professional (or personal) success in the way that you could if you said, "can," "maybe," and "yes."

Words define our behavior. Since our words come to us from somewhere deep in our subconscious thoughts, if we change how we think, we can change our words/language, and finally alter our behavior. Positive self-talk is a great way to start re-programming your mindset. If you tell yourself everyday that "yes, I can," then you can bet you will succeed. This is an easy thing to do when you are by yourself or even with others. You can do it verbally or silently. For instance, every night you might want to say three affirmations before going to sleep: *I am a healthy and happy person. I am enjoying my true life's work. I am a capable and competent person with many talents to share.* Or if you are in a crowd and you are beginning to think your typical negative thoughts: "I never know the right thing to say," "I sound so stupid," "I am not as smart as they are, no one will want to talk with me," etc, literally, bite your tongue! This will remind you to STOP what you are thinking so that you can immediately think positive thoughts: *"I am an intelligent, creative person." "Anybody would be lucky to talk with me tonight!"* Try it, the results will be amazing!

In addition to our mental programming, we have also learned ways to act and behave through our life experiences. For instance, in your childhood you may have been taught or allowed to be dependent, lazy, or not to take the lead. If so, you may need to work on some of your deeply ingrained beliefs about what others should do for you. Are they appropriate given today's circumstances? Has the way you acted in past work-related settings been effective? Keep in mind that we are free to write our biographies, our own life scripts. If you don't like the one you've been living thus far, throw it out and write a new one today! If you have always wanted to travel across country in a van, become a rock climber, move to another country, work for the movie industry, whatever! Don't just think about it, do it! *Why* are you waiting? *What* are you waiting for? *Who* are you waiting for? Get out of your own way and get to it. In the book, *7 Habits of Highly Successful People,* Dr. Stephen Covey says:

> *In developing our own self awareness, many of us discover ineffective scripts, deeply imbedded habits that are totally unworthy of us, totally incongruent with the things we really value in life . . . We don't have to live with those scripts. We are responsible to use our imagination and creativity to write new ones that are more effective, more congruent with our deepest values and with the correct principles that give our values meaning.*

Our associations with others often give us feedback on what we are like, but can sometimes be a distorted picture of ourselves. Our life scripts come from the people that impact us the most and even from those we barely know. First and foremost, our families teach us about ourselves. But remember: many families are dysfunctional and often do not do a good job of encouraging, enlightening, or loving. Many times parents and children do not take the time to really get to know one another. And even after you grow up, parents tend to treat their adult children as if they were still twelve years old. But, at some point in your life, maybe even today, you need to reject anything negative others have said about you. Take it upon yourself to write your own *life script.* I truly believe that if you see yourself as a positive, productive, confident, competent person, then others will see you that way too.

Besides our family, friends, co-workers, and acquaintances, the most significant person who contributes to our life scripts is our life mate. He or she has a lot to do with our self-esteem, level of personal satisfaction, and ability to grow and develop. If they are a negative influence in our life, then they will provide limiting beliefs. The more time we spend with someone, the greater their impact. So, if after day after day, month after month, year after year you have been with someone who has communicated to you that: "you are no good," "nobody would want to hire you," "you could not make it without me" then you are going to start believing it.

What do you aspire to be? Your aspirations are your aims, goals, and desires, which are actually the possibilities of your life. Set your sights high and believe that you can achieve what you dream about. Keep a positive frame of mind.

Your state of mind is created by what you think about. If you think negatively, you form feelings of indecision, doubt, and fear which only lead to chaos and confusion. Every thought, word, action returns to you. What you put out is what you get back. You must take responsibility for what you want and become disciplined in your thoughts and actions. Since thoughts create reality, you must monitor yours and turn them around to be positive. In the words of Benjamin Disraeli, *"As you think, so shall you be."* What do you think about all day long? Do you think that you can do the things you want to do? Or do you blow out your dreams with negative thinking?

Control your thoughts lest they control you. The power of positive thinking is based on the fact that our thoughts radiate out to find their corresponding experience. What you hold in your mind is drawn to you because you believe what you think and then act on that belief to fulfill your own prophecy. In other words, you confirm your own thoughts. If you *think you are going to succeed, you will.* Likewise, if you think (unconsciously or consciously) that *you are going to fail, you will.* You can (and must) change your programming with positive affirmations. To create an effective affirmation, phrase them in present tense, repeat them with a positive tone, use powerful, motivating words, and keep them short. A good affirmation should say what your soul needs to hear.

Sample Affirmations

I am a creation of Spirit, as such I am blessed with the power of creation. I create the work that I want to do and the life I want to live effortlessly and joyfully.

My life's work is now ready for me and I for it. I perform my work lovingly and share myself wholly with others. I am a success in my personal and professional life.

Look Within For the Answers

John Locke was observant when he said, *"The thoughts that come often unsought, as it were, drop into the mind, are commonly the most valuable we have."* Why? Because those thoughts are the ones with the best information—the information that is meant just for us. We will be happier in our life if we can develop the skill of looking within. Unfortunately, we have not been taught how to live our lives in accordance with our own natures. We look outside of ourselves for answers to our questions, when we should be looking within. When you begin to live in awareness, you will find that you move along your path with ease and grace. By trusting yourself and that you are being led in the right direction, your life will become lighter and more joyful.

The key is to get in touch with your inner self and fully acknowledge the intuitive power that you have. If you know who you really are and what your life purpose is, the bumps and forks in the road can be taken in easy stride. But if you are not sure about who you are or why you are here, then even small decisions become daunting—like mountains instead of molehills. When your heart tells you to do something, you must simply do it. By being who you naturally are, your path is obvious and uncluttered. When you let your natural self take the lead, you will find your destiny, including your right work, the right relationship, the right life. The best will come to you, if you let it.

We have gotten too far away from our inner nature. As a society, we mainly focus on the physical world, and have forgotten how to access our metaphysical one. We make decisions from the ego, instead of the soul. When we become more enlightened, we will begin to see the spiritual significance in our everyday decisions. As we look within, we must ask ourselves what it is that we most want to do in life. We must recognize what we want, ask for it, and be open to receiving it. We need to knock in order for the doors of opportunity to be opened. Because as long as our deepest dreams and wildest passions lay dormant, we will not be able to access them. It is as though our life purpose is on a hard drive that has a special password. The password is simply to declare it to ourselves, and then to others. If we do not bring our desires to our consciousness, we will not be able to manifest them. The first thing to do is to see the possibilities in your mind's eye, then you will be able to create them in your life. You also need to learn to balance taking action(ego) and allowing nature to run its course (Spirit).

Your nature is your greatest strength. Do what you are naturally good at. When you are giving your gifts and doing your right work, you attract people, circumstances and resources necessary to succeed. However, the way of nature also means embracing insecurity and imperfection! Nature is far from perfect, and we as humans, are far from perfect, too. It is this imperfection that makes our gifts so unique.

The nature of all human beings, like flowers, is to bloom—to be big, beautiful works of art. Carl Jung agrees, *"Follow that will and that way which experience confirms to be your own."* When you follow your nature, like a great river, it guides you to your life purpose.

If you don't follow your nature, you will not likely experience the life that was meant for you. In fact, bottled creative energy is a great source of stress and anxiety. "Psyche" is the Greek word for soul. When we are doing work or other things that go against our nature, our psyches/souls are affected. We don't feel right, whole.

Abraham Maslow said, *"A musician must make his music, an artist must paint, a poet must write if he is to ultimately be at peace with himself."* To NOT do the thing you have to do is a major reasons people feel frustrated. I know that when I don't follow my nature, (such as when my nature calls me to write) I become uncomfortable— I am struggling/resisting myself. I must follow it where it leads, and I often do not know the direction, but still I must go. I have also learned to follow my nature in other work-related situations, if something is not going well for me, or my values are called into question, then I listen to what my inner self tells me to do. It has always worked for me.

In Eastern cultures, people are very aware of their life force energy, which is known as "ch'i." The purpose of "ch'i" is to circulate energy to bring about spiritual, emotional and physical health. When your life energy is freely flowing, you experience joy. When it is blocked, you experience pain. Since Americans by and large are not taught to "tune-in" to their body vibrations, many people feel stuck in jobs that hold little or no meaning for them. Their life force is not flowing, and this creates negative energy in our work force.

We go against our nature in so many ways. I do not believe it is natural for human beings to be unhappy in work or stressed out all the time. We have temporarily forgotten who we truly are and keep driving ourselves in this consumer-oriented society to acquire more and more stuff, thinking that is what will make us happy, and that is what life is all about. But we are slowly waking to the knowledge that Spirit is always present. We are coming to know our full divinity—we are already wired for greatness and waking up to the knowledge that there is work that is meant just for us. All we have to do is to tap into our internal, universal database.

We need more spirited work. William Elery Channing said, *"Every human being is intended to have a character of his own, to be what no other is, and to do what no other can do."* Inspired works of art or everyday chores come from being "in spirit." The word "inspired" means to *breathe into, to communicate divine instruction to, to infuse ideas or poetic spirit into, to "animate" in general.* It means to make something come alive, to infuse spirit into your work. I do not think it is difficult to see that we need more inspired work in our society. There is a frightening amount of low quality, meaningless work on the market. When we perform work strictly for economic reasons instead of spiritual ones, the product or outcome is devoid of love and spirit. We need more educational, humanistic, inspired work! Let's all start creating movies, books, businesses, homes, schools that are designed to enlighten our mind, body, and spirit!

13 Behaviors That Will Prevent You From Creating Your Life's Work

1) **Doubt**

Doubt is a powerful and negative thought. Since thoughts create reality, your ability to think positively will impact your ability to create your life's work. If you doubt that you will find your true vocation, you most likely won't. Because you have already made up your mind, you will not act in ways that will open the doors of opportunity.

2)   **Idealistic Thinking**
There are no perfect positions, but there may be quite a few jobs that you would enjoy doing and could make you happy. However, if you believe that there is only one perfect career for you—you will never be satisfied with the work at hand. Idealistic thinking can lead you on a wild goose chase—forever job hunting.

3)   **Not Taking One's Life Seriously**
When you choose to take a passive approach to work, you tend to fall into one unfulfilling position after another. Your life is serious business. You must treat your own career as a business and become committed to creating the work you want to do.

4)   **Lack of Awareness**
You cannot start the creation process without first knowing who you really are—your knowledge, skills, and abilities. You have to do some soul searching before you can begin creating your life's work. Unaware people apply for jobs or positions that they are really not qualified for or really don't want. Focus your efforts on what you really *want* to do. When you focus and put your energy into the right direction, opportunities will unfold in unexpected ways.

5)   **Failure to Know Who Your Potential Employers/Customers Are**
If you try mass marketing to random people, your results will be dismal. Take the time to get to know who could benefit from your services, build a strong relationship with them, and you will always be marketable and employable.

6)   **Poor Decision-Making Skills**
If you have not mastered Get Smart! decision-making, you may keep making poor career choices. You need to develop your deci-

sion-making skills before you can create your life's work. Remember that if you place yourself in positions that are not a good fit, your chances of finding the right career greatly decrease.

7)   **Your Ego**
Our egos often get in the way of finding our true calling because they prevent us from looking at the world through anyone else's eyes but our own. We need to realize that the world does not revolve around us and that the things we do affect others. The ego also mistakenly focuses on external rewards such as money or prestige when making a career decision. Do not let your over-blown ego get in the way of your work.

8)   **Mad Marketing**
Do not use ineffective methods of marketing. What does this mean? Using sloppy, unfocused, unprofessional materials. Take the time to develop professional, error-free materials to send to people. This may be your only chance to impress them. Remember, too, that you must not only use traditional methods of marketing, but also try different techniques, especially those related to technology.

9)   **Bad Attitude**
You have to maintain a positive mental attitude throughout the creating process. Having the right attitude can make all the difference in the world. Because thoughts create reality, we must not only think but also *believe* that what we want to do is possible and within our reach. And our reach should exceed our grasp.

10)   **Lack of Preparation**
It's been said, *"If you fail to plan, you plan to fail."* This is very true when it comes to career development. One day, before you know it, your dream may start to manifest itself. You have to be prepared for it or you may miss out or wait too long to act. You have to be ready and willing to do what is necessary to make your dreams come true. All it takes is a little preparation (and perspiration).

11)   **Lack of Organizational Skills**
Keep yourself organized, have a file system that works for you, know where to get information when you need it. If this is not your strong suit, hire a personal assistant.

12)   **Lack of Commitment to Yourself or Your Career**
If you are not committed, you will not work hard. Contrary to popular belief, dreams do not happen for the lucky few, dreams are lived out by people who actively work hard to make them happen. They persist, put in the effort, believe in themselves, and are committed to the process.

13)   **Refusal to Change**
If you have been trying the same things as long as you can remember, with little or no real results, it is time to make a change. It is not healthy to go through life inflexible and unwilling to grow and develop. As your life circumstances change, learn to cope and adapt so that you always have something positive to contribute to your work.

Journal Assignment #4
What limiting beliefs have you held regarding your career? How have they hindered your professional development? What affirmations can you replace them with that will inspire you in those moments of doubt?

Chapter Four

Get in Touch With Your Spirit

"Each path is only one of a million paths.
Look at each path very carefully and deliberately and ask yourself one
question: Does this path have heart? If it does, then the path is good.
If it doesn't, it is of no use."

—Don Juan

Holistic Living/Working

We are now in a new century, the Age of Aquarius. What an exciting time to be alive. Some "free thinkers" have proposed that along with many other societal changes, such as radical changes in technology and in the environment, human beings will undergo a transformation in their consciousness. In the Age of Enlightenment, we will take notice, understand, and become more aware of our lives than ever before. Because our world is entering into another time in history, it makes sense that people will learn to live and work in ways that are for the greatest and highest good.

There are millions of people today who practice a progressive way of living and working. They try to live life holistically by integrating the many parts of their lives. They understand that each part of their "life pie" is just as essential as other parts, and that if one is out of alignment, such as the work "piece," that it affects the other pieces. People who truly practice holistic living know that each piece of their "life pie" is equally as delicious as the others. In terms of living out your life here on earth, what does all that mean? Perhaps that you need to take a close look at what really matters to you. Is one area taking up too much room? Do you need to increase the size of one your smaller pieces?

Holistic living attempts to incorporate healthy and "whole" living through taking care of our minds, bodies and souls. In modern society, this may mean different things to different people. No doubt this will continue to be the norm for the future. In fact, individuals will define for themselves what is important and essential to their well being. But for most, there will be a need to find some sort of spirituality, something to connect them to life. People of the enlightened era are seeking a higher source of power. As a result, more emphasis will be placed on other ways of knowing and unscientific ways of explaining and understanding what life in this world is all about. Currently there is rising interest in astrology, natural medicines/healing, massage therapy, and other forms of natural, yet unexplainable phenomenon. We are also becoming more interested in and accepting of the unexplainable, such as hypnosis, holistic medicine and meditation.

In order to live a complete and whole life, we must develop all of our life dimensions, (love, labor, leisure, and learning) and we must ascend to a higher level of consciousness. "Human wellness" can be defined as an evolving and growing process of all aspects of life—emotional, intellectual, psychological, physical, work, spiritual and health. Honestly assess your current level of wholeness. Are you balanced? Do your life areas complement, contrast, or contradict one another? Do you spend a majority of your time in one over the other, for example, valuing work over your spiritual or love life? If not, ask yourself which one is out of alignment? Stimulation from each area of your life is essential to maintaining an appropriate internal/spiritual balance.

Smart Tip
➡ We can learn to integrate mind-body-spirit when we have a daily and disciplined practice such as prayer, yoga, meditation, journaling, etc.

Get Smart!
➡ Striving for personal balance is of the utmost importance in stiving to achieve a healthy, holistic lifestyle.

Journal Assignment #5
There are four major life dimensions: Love, Labor, Learning, and Leisure. Consider how actively involved you are in each of these. Draw your life pie and the size of each of your pieces. Write in detail how each of these roles is

either fulfilled or unfulfilled in your own life. Do they complement or compete for your wholeness? Is it possible that one aspect is a detriment to the rest?

Know Your Spiritual Self

Of all the aspects of our life, spirituality is the one that is most overlooked in our current, hectic modern world. This will hopefully change during this century, but in order for you to prepare for this coming transformation, you must first look within yourself for the answers to your life questions. The Tao says, *"If you want to find life, look inside you."* I would expand on this and say," *If you want to find your life's work, look inside you."* As life and work are so inextricably linked, you cannot fully experience one without the other.

As a spiritual being you are filled with life and love. It is up to you to get in touch with that part of yourself. *You must awaken to the realization that you are a spiritual being having a human experience.* You can do this through meditative and reflective activities. Someone with spiritual wellness strives for personal growth and is willing to experience and find truths about life, wants inner peace, strength and love, willingly evaluates personal values, and acts and lives in a manner that suggest humanity is a vital part of the greater whole.

Do you feel as if your life has meaning and purpose? Do you feel connected to others and to a higher power? Do you accept and understand your place in the universe? Are you in touch with your spiritual nature? Do you know what moves you, brings you joy, or fills you with passion? Do you know, accept, understand, and love *you?* Do you lead your life according to your intuitive guidance?

If you answered "yes" to these questions, you should feel extremely blessed as you have discovered what most people have missed—a sense of who you really are and how you fit into the world. If not, don't despair. You can develop your spirituality and experience the kind of career that you deserve. The first step in discovering your spiritual self is knowing *who you really are.* I realize this sounds very easy, but I want you to really stop and think about it. Do you really know who you are? What makes you happy? What makes you excited to be alive?

Journal Assignment #6

Do this section in free-form. Just start writing, no editing allowed, so that you can truly delve into your soul. Title this entire section: "My Spiritual Self"

Write exactly who you think you are. This can be as creative as you want it to be. It can be descriptive words, short sentences, a detailed paragraph, anything. Write as much as you can for as long as you can. And afterwards, read what you've written. What did you learn about yourself? Does some of what you wrote come as a surprise to you?

Again write in free-form:

What inspires you?

What do you believe in?

What are you passionate about?

What is essential to you?

Finally, what do you think your life purpose is—what were you put on this earth to do?

Many great thinkers of our time have struggled with these kinds of questions in order to find themselves, to know themselves. Know that you are not alone in this process of self-discovery. The psychologist Victor Frankl, in *Man's Search for Meaning* shares his experiences of living through the Holocaust, but somehow manages to find meaning in his life. He said, *"Everyone has his own specific vocation or mission in life to carry out a concrete assignment which demands fulfillment. Therein he cannot be replaced, nor can his life be repeated. Therein, everyone's task is as unique as his specific opportunity to implement it."* He certainly demonstrated his own belief system, as he survived imprisonment and went on to develop logotherapy, a therapy technique that helps people discover their personal meaning. Likewise, each of us has a purpose, a point. We all matter. We all have things to teach, knowledge to gain, love to share, lives to lead. It is your responsibility to find out what you have to offer the world.

Spirituality and Work

Spirituality is more than an identification or association with a particular religion or religious beliefs. It is more than just believing in God. It is about our connection and relationship with nature, each other, and Spirit. Spirituality is a way of life and is individually defined and experienced by each human being. Spirituality gives many people a sense of the inter-relatedness of life and its inhabitants, it helps people feel whole and provides us a sense of meaning. The poet Yeats once defined spirituality as, *"The core of the person—the center from which meaning, self, and life understanding are generated."*

For far too long, people have believed that our job/position /title was our source, instead of a vehicle to be able to live life as we choose to. In fact, we are in a partnership with a higher power, who is the true source; however, we have to open to this truth in order to receive all that is available to us.

Case Illustration

Brian is a man in his forties, who held a very important job (according to society's standards). He was a doctor. He had a wife and two children, and a seemingly satisfying life. But Brian had felt a longing to do something different with his life for many years. He yearned for a simpler, less stressful lifestyle. One day after twenty years in his profession, he left it all behind to search for the real meaning in his life. He left his family and home in search of himself, his Spirit. Alone, he traveled for six months and then came back home, sold his house and various belongings. He then became a candle maker. His new-found sense of spirituality led him to create a different way of making money, and a lighter way of living. He now travels around the country with his wife selling his wares and is finally content and at peace with himself. He learned that the source of his happiness did not come from having an important, high-paying job, but rather an important, meaningful life.

In the realm of work, there seems to be a connection to meaningful work and those who are in touch with their spiritual selves. The rising interest in spirituality and its importance will impact the modern world of work in that it will allow us to create new work that provides a sense of meaning and allows us to express our Spirit. One aspect of spirituality and work that is evolving is a new definition of balance. New age workers do not want to spend all their time working. In fact, they are seeking more enjoyment from "the business of living."

As we move further into the 21st century, more career options will continue to be available to a more diverse workforce. At the same time, people of all backgrounds are realizing that whole life balance is important to true success. If you want to create your true life's work, you have to look at your life in its entirety, and realize how each of the different areas of life impact each other. If you choose a career that fits in and complements the other dimensions, you will experience more overall fulfillment.

To uncover your purpose, you must get in touch with your inner self, pay attention to that small inner voice that whispers to you its need to create, take action on this information, and then manifest it in the world. This will lead you to create work that you love to do. And as a result, people will pay you for it. Having money allows you to do more of the things that you love to do in your spare time. And it gives you the freedom of when, where, and how you choose to work.

As a society, we have foolishly believed in the lack and scarcity paradigm; "there is not enough to go around," and that "you have to fight for your fair share." In the era of enlightenment, we will believe in the abundance of the universe—that there is plenty for all. In our world, money is a means to an end in that it allows us to do what we want to do. Contrary to popular belief, financial abundance is something everyone is worthy and deserving of. But we have many psychological blocks that prevent us from believing this. What few people realize is that money is a source of energy, thus our beliefs about it will be reflected in how much we share and save. Again, thoughts create reality. If you believe that money is good and that you are worthy of it, you will attract financial abundance into your life. Likewise, if you believe that creating your life's work is good, and that you are worthy of it, you will attract career abundance into your life. By taking a proactive, smart approach to your life/career planning, you can experience abundance in all the areas of your life.

You Are a Creative Spirit

As humans, we have two soul purposes. *The first is the universal soul purpose: to remember who we really are—Love. And the second is a unique soul purpose: to play a role better or differently than any other soul in a given lifetime.* When you find your unique purpose, and are able to express love through your work, it becomes easier to live out your universal purpose. Amazingly, when you live your life based on your vision and your purpose, the universe supports you by providing information, resources, and energy.

As humans, we have an inherent ability to create. Our God-given gift is life. What we do with it remains our own responsibility. But one thing we must do is *create*. Creation is the basis of human life. It is our nature to create—whether it is building, writing, painting, designing, communicating, etc. As humans we express our inner spiritual natures by our outer (physical) creations. Sadly, modern men and women feel spiritually lost, disconnected and discontented. They can turn resentful toward themselves, others, and even "God," all because they have not discovered their unique purpose, their soul's full potential. It is our society's unimaginable loss if its citizens become bored, depressed, or feel unworthy of meaningful work because those same folks will find unhealthy ways to feel alive (acts of destruction are still acts of creation). This is why great works of art, (as well as street grafitti) have much to tell us about what is going on inside the creator's heart and mind. This is usually a result of their innate need to feel engaged with not only themselves, but with others. Grown adults, just like children will "act out" to get this attention.

Humanity's work is to evolve by learning to love more fully. And a person's individual purpose is to do the work they were meant to do. This is why so many people suffer a loss of identity when they lose a job. Without work, they are not sure what to do with themselves or who they are. Meaningful work helps us to feel that our existence matters, that we fit into the world. This is paradoxical because our souls need to perform work, yet we are just as love-able and valuable as spirits even if we didn't work. However, as humans we need to put ourselves to work—we need to feel we are contributing and have worth.

You can become a great creator by catching on fire with your ideas and being enthusiastic. Enthusiasm means *"possessed by God."* Enthusiasm is contagious, energizes you and provides you with vital energy to accomplish all things. People who perform their work in a loving, enthusiastic way approach their tasks/duties in a joyful spirit whatever the work is that they are doing. If we want a healthier society, we first have to let our Spirit express itself in a meaningful way. The simple truth is when people are contributing, they feel worthy, when they are not contributing, they feel worthless. Every person needs to create and share something with others, no matter how big or small. Whether that means someone who finds the cure for cancer, or the custodian who cleans the medical facility. Each soul has to give of him or herself to others. Without that, there is a disconnect from our life force, which in turn becomes a disconnect from society.

Get Smart!
➡ We have the opportunity to leave our world in a better state for our children's children. How can you contribute?

The Power of Passion, the Agony of Pursuit

Passion is what you feel inspired by, what makes your eyes light up, what makes your heart beat a little faster. Feeling passion for someone or something is easy. Choosing to pursue it is hard. This is because following your passion involves taking a risk vs. staying secure. Many times we think we can't or shouldn't do what we really love to do because it seems too self-indulgent. The truth is that our passions are ours because they are meant to be experienced and enjoyed by us.

With your recognition comes the inner conflict of the practical vs. impractical. On the practical side, your mind will tell you why you should or should not do something. On the impractical side, your heart tells you to go for it no matter what. Bringing balance to these two faculties empowers you to make smarter decisions. Ultimately, when creating your life's work, you seek ways to apply your natural gifts and talents. But what if you are a very passionate person with many gifts and talents? Do you have to give one up for the other? Not at all! In fact, why not combine your passions into meaningful work? For example, take a person who loves animals and graphic design. That person could market herself as a graphic designer who specializes in animal-related companies and causes.

What if you don't feel passionate about anything in particular? If you are not sure what your passions are, you may have to do some soul-searching to uncover dormant dreams and long-lost passions. We all have them. A good place to start is to look within, which is where passion lives. Passions can come from the on-going lessons and obstacles you have had to overcome or they can be the things that you do when time seems to fly. Look back over your life, and you will be surprised that, with a little reflection, thoughts, ideas and images spring up from your childhood, reminding you of what you loved to do as a child. What did you pretend to be or say you would be when you were growing up?

In romance, a passionate embrace usually leads to the next step in love-making. When you finally embrace what you are passionate about, you will find that you are forced to take action. Embraced by passion, you are compelled to continue with the process. Loving what you do brings you joy which leads to creation. Anything that comes from joy or love has to be worthwhile. While passion is what we feel, pursuit is what we do. The reason we say "pursuing a career" is because it takes continuous effort and action. What idea can you embrace and move forward? Let yourself go, because like e.e. cummings who said, *"In time of daffodils who know the goal of living is to grow, forgetting why, remember how."* You, like a flower— who knows it's only duty is to bloom—once you find out what you are meant to do, you will start to bloom in unexpected directions.

Lance Morrow once said, *"Work is the way we tend the world, the way people connect. It is the most vigorous, vivid sign of life—in individuals and in civilization."* Humanity's mission is to help create a more loving, peaceful and enlightened world. You can play your part by achieving your universal and unique purpose. To tap into your own divinity, you have to let your soul stir you up a bit, get upset, and feel passionate about things. Emotions lead to motion. If we have faith in God or Spirit, we can call forth our gifts and become a force for good in the world.

Your presence is your present. Everyone has gifts to share. When you are giving your gifts, Spirit is reaching through you and touching others. Think of a teacher or doctor, or anyone who is sharing themselves with others through their work. We can also find our true work by becoming *open.* Our ego does not know what is best for us, but our soul does. If we can listen to it, we can find our work naturally and easily. It is when we feed into our ego's needs that we get side-tracked and lost.

Once you have uncovered your inner core, the essence of who you are, your life will naturally unfold, often in unexpected, more enjoyable directions. At this stage of career development, you do not need to know or expend energy on how your dreams will play themselves out or how you will create your life's work. In fact, the hard part is done—you know what you are meant to do. Enjoy!

Unleash Your Creativity

Julia Cameron once said, *"Our creative dreams and yearnings come from a divine source. As we move toward our dreams, we move toward our divinity."* And it is true. You will become more divine as you become more creative. Creativity is loving what you do no matter how menial or small the task. You find intrinsic value in the act—such as gardening, painting, or cooking. Creativity is the quality that you bring to the activity you are doing. It is an attitude, an inner approach to how you look at things.

Being creative is not limited to activities traditionally thought of as "creative," such as painting, writing, composing, or dancing. Everyone can be creative, even when doing simple chores. Do not limit yourself and narrowly define creativity, as I did for a very long time. I can remember back to the first grade when I drew a picture of the sky and colored it purple. I was very proud of my landscape. To me, it was beautiful and perfect, but the teacher criticized me in front of the class, saying, "The sky is not purple, it is blue." I was devastated. I could not understand what was wrong with my sky; or for that matter, what was wrong with me. From that day on, I never thought of myself as "creative." It has only been during the past few years that I have realized I am very creative, in the way I write, the way I think, the way I am!

Whether or not we consider ourselves *artists,* we are all in the business of creating our lives. Each of us is here to contribute something unique, yet most of us aren't sure what that "something" is. We would like life to be more beautiful, but don't think there is anything *we* can do. Yet, a simple creative act enhances the beauty of the world. Just think about how you feel when you see an architecturally beautiful skyscraper, or colorful downtown mural, or exquisitely cared for garden. Each of these works is a work of creativity, a work of art. Creative work can help us to heal our planet and our souls.

The reality is that we are born creators. *Just to be* is to be creative. But to make the conscious choice to act on your ideas and thoughts is truly powerful. You have only to watch children, especially at play, to see the creative force in its purest, most exuberant form. But along the way, we squelch their imagination. We teach them that there is "right" and "wrong" way to do things. We also instill in them that other people are the authority—that they can't trust themselves. Albert Einstein once said, *"Imagination is more powerful than knowledge."* But in our society, we promote the collection of knowledge instead of the expansion of our imaginations.

Creativity is associated with a kind of intelligence— the ability to take notice and act upon the nuances of nature. An artist has his eyes, ears, nose, heart, and mind wide open—this heightened awareness enables them to tune in to their thought patterns, which guides their work. The first step to unleashing your creativity is to *start* the process. For example, if you want to become a writer, you will not succeed until you start writing. Putting pen to paper is the first step in the creative process. Now, what you write first may not be the final draft, (believe me, it won't!) but it is a vital component to unleashing the creator within. If you are having difficulty coming up with ideas, instead of trying to force them, relax. Slow down and allow your inner self to give you guidance. And it is very, very important not to judge yourself for not getting it "right" or perfect, because that will definitely dampen your creative spirit.

Creativity is a process of unfoldment, leading you to the next stage, in that each thing you do leads you to a deeper level of understanding, emotion, and thought. The Get Smart! creativity process involve the use of both sides of the brain, the analytical side and the artistic side.

The first stage occurs in the right-brain—*insight,*
where you have a flash, a hunch or intuition about an idea.
The second stage occurs in the left-brain—*reflection,*
where you analyze the idea.
The third stage occurs in the right-brain—*imagination,*
where you generate ideas about the original idea.
The fourth stage occurs in the left-brain—*evaluation,*
where you analyze the feasibility of all the ideas generated.
The Four Roles of the creative process, according to Roger von Oech, author of *A Kick in the Seat of the Pants:*

The Explorer: Searches for materials with which
to make new ideas.
(He breaks his routine and gets out there to explore).
The Artist: Takes the materials and transforms them
into original ideas.
(She imagines and reflects about the idea).
The Judge: Takes on the evaluative role, and decides what to

do with the idea: implement it, modify it, or discard it.
(He considers what the idea is trying to do and sees
the possibilities).
The Warrior: Takes action on the idea.
(She prepares for criticism and gets back up
when knocked down).

What creative role are you playing? How can you move to the next level/stage in the creative process?

Journal Assignment #7

Invite yourself to be creative. Draw a life map, highlighting the major accomplishments and disappointments in your life. What are the themes? What does your Spirit need to say or do in this lifetime? What is the "it" that you must do? (Paint it, teach it, write it, sing it, develop it?) What is your life trying to tell you to create?

Chapter Five

Living By Vision, Working With Purpose

"Dream lofty dreams, as you dream, so shall you become.
Your vision is the promise of what you shall one day be;
your ideal is the prophecy of what you shall at last unveil."
—James Allen

Whole Life Planning

Like William Henley who once said, *"I am the master of my fate. The captain of my soul,"* I agree that Life is a Do-It Yourself project. If you want to live a certain kind of life, you are going to have to be proactive so you can consciously create life as you would like it. You must first mentally visualize and then physically create what you want. You can do this by having a clear vision and developing strong intentions. Your life is your gift, how you appreciate it and use it is entirely up to you. Take this story as an example of the importance of building it with excellence and pride (author unknown):

An elderly carpenter was ready to retire. He told his employer-contractor of his plans to leave the house-building business and live a more leisurely life with his wife enjoying his extended family. He would miss the paycheck, but he needed to retire. They could get by.

The contractor was sorry to see his good worker go and asked if he could build just one more house as a personal favor. The carpenter said yes, but in time it was easy to see that his heart was not in his work. He resorted to shoddy workmanship and used inferior materials. It was an unfortu-

nate way to end a dedicated career.

When the carpenter finished his work, the employer came to inspect the house. He handed the front-door key to the carpenter. "This is your house," he said, "my gift to you." The carpenter was shocked! What a shame! If he had only known he was building his own house, he would have done it all so differently.

So it is with us. We build our lives, a day at a time, often putting less than our best into the building. Then we are shocked to realize we have to live in the house we have built! If we could do it over, we'd do it much differently. And better.

But you cannot go back. You are the carpenter. Each day you hammer a nail, place a board, or erect a wall. Your attitudes and the choices you make today build the house you live in tomorrow. Build wisely! Build with commitment, pride, joy, and love.

When planning our future, we need to look at our whole life, and each of its dimensions. Stephen Covey once said, *"Begin with the end in mind."* To build the life and career you want, you must first have a vision—first visualize, then crystallize. Anyone can get a job, but what we are concerned with is a much greater goal than that. We are talking about creating our life's work, and that involves risk, energy, and perseverance. Considering our whole life areas (love, labor, leisure, and learning) when consciously creating our vision enables us to express who we really are and allows us to live a fuller life. In all areas, we need to feel that we have power to direct and create the kind of life we desire.

A vision is a guiding image or blueprint of success formed in terms of how you want to live your life. It is a picture of the preferred future that you seek to create. Your vision reveals what you really want out of life and empowers you to make smarter life decisions. A well-written vision statement should inspire you, be clear and concrete, stretch your imagination, and support your value system. You can evoke your vision with imagery, meditation, symbols, journaling, and story telling.

Think big. In fact, if your vision doesn't scare you, then either your vision or your Spirit is too small. The power of belief in what you want can take you far. When you finally, truly **make up your mind** about something, it is much easier to do than you first thought. It is all the going back and forth, coming up with reasons to do it or not to do it, thinking and talking about it that makes it difficult for most people to put great ideas into action. The power of your thinking is limitless. No matter what problem or situation you are faced with, you can put your mind over the matter and more effectively deal with it.

When you are planning your career, you have to keep a clear vision of what you want, otherwise, you will wake up five or twenty years down the road and wonder "How did I get here?" You are in charge of your life. You can create the work and life experiences you want. For instance, if you want to spend more time helping others on the job, or do more project management, create it in the job you already have. If that is not possible, you can manifest it elsewhere. Above all, if you are not happy doing what you are doing, stop! No one is making you do it but yourself.

Case Illustration

I will share with you how my company, Get Smart! LearningBooks & Seminars, came to be. Several years ago, I was working at a for-profit university as Director of Career Development. I enjoyed my work very much, especially the students, and had no real plans to change career directions, let alone start my own business. As with any organization, there were politics and ethical dilemmas. Suffice it to say, my personal values were in direct conflict with that of the company for a variety of reasons.

I also hadn't planned on writing my first book Get Smart! About Modern Romantic Relationships, but had started writing it while working there. I soon found myself working so many hours that I did not have time to complete my passion-project. As it came to be, I did leave the school and took about five months to do nothing but put the finishing touches on the book. As I became more enmeshed in my writing, the Get Smart! concept evolved. I began teaching Get Smart! Seminars based on my book, and soon was receiving all kinds of contracts for other training projects. Now, I am my own boss, and in charge of the work that I take on. I also have a very clear vision of where I am headed. Does what I do have meaning? More than I could have imagined. The really amazing thing is that after I made the transition, things started to fall in place— work and support came from unexpected people and places. I believe that this will happen for all of you, if you can just learn to follow your intuition and be willing to take risks.

What Vision Do You Have For Your Life?

A life vision (also known as a mission statement) is not just the work you want to do, it is the underlying motivator to why you do what you do in *all areas of your life*. It is built around your most important values and beliefs. It is a guiding document in which you can refer to throughout your life.

How you create your life based on your vision is how you will consciously choose to live your life. Choose wisely, as each area impacts others. For example, if you are not living your vision in one of your areas, such as *labor*, it will impact how you experience your other life areas. The goal is to strive for your unique balance. In fact, when you find your unique balance, each life dimension complements and supports the others. For example, a healthy leisure life where you can relax and become refreshed enhances your love, labor, and learning areas.

Some benefits of writing a life vision are that it identifies your direction, promotes laser-like focus, encourages creative thinking, and results in more fulfilling life. As Joel Arthur Blake commented, *"Vision without action is merely a dream, action without vision just passes the time. Vision with action can change the world."* By writing out your life vision, you will have a clearer idea of where you are going, which will later help you develop a strategy on how to get there. Look at your life in its entirety and actively reflect about how you want it to be and the person you want to become. This will help you to choose work, people, and situations that are best suited to you.

Living by your life vision will make it easier to stay on your spiritual path because you will know what is important to you, and feel empowered to develop a strategy. Sometimes you will feel scared, uncertain, and at those times, you need to tap into your intuition for guidance. Believe in yourself. You can do anything you set your mind and heart on.

And remember, you are free to create your life vision however you wish it to be. Because it comes from your soul, your vision will no doubt be what you hold closest to your heart. Writing a life vision will help you to recognize the importance of taking a proactive stance when *designing* your life. Just like a builder who builds a house, who develops a blueprint first, your life vision is your blueprint. People with clear life visions do not merely react to whatever life throws at them, but instead, actively participate in creating the way they want their lives to be. That is because they are in tune with their higher selves and they choose not to cater to the needs of their lower selves (ego). Ask yourself: Is my life progressing the way I would like it?

Rate your current life circumstance in the following dimensions:
Love_____   Labor_____   Leisure_____   Learning_____

3:    I am living in alignment with my life vision
2:    I am mostly living in alignment with my life vision
1:    I am somewhat living in alignment with my life vision
0:    I am not living in alignment with my life vision

If you scored:
9-12:   You are in alignment
5-8:   You are not far off, with some adjustments,
        you can be in alignment
0-4:   You are out of alignment

In addition to having various experiences, we also play many roles within each of our life areas. Let's use the example of a woman in her mid-forties:

Love: Mother, wife, sister, child, friend
Labor: Teacher and writer in the creative arts
Leisure: Tennis player, traveler, beachcomber
Learning: College-educated, lifelong learner

The vision she wrote for herself gives her a clear idea of what she wants to experience while on her journey. Once she knows what she values, she can then set specific goals for each of her life areas.

Life Vision Visualization

During meditation, visualize your whole life. Think about each dimension. Create a special place, where you can focus on the kind of life you want to create—decorate it with symbols of success, etc. When you do your meditation, you may want to light a candle and play soft music to set the mood. You also may want to combine this exercise with a daily affirmation. Release these positive thoughts and images to the universe and let go of the outcome.

Close your eyes, take five cleansing breaths, visualize a peaceful and calming place that you like to spend time—perhaps a favorite vacation spot, the mountains or the beach. Look around you, and take in the environment, listen to the sounds, feel how you feel being there. Finally, find a comfortable place to rest. Now, slowly relax your entire body and mind and let your mind wander to thoughts of the kind of life you would like to live. Imagine everything in your head.

What would your love-life be like?

What kind of work would you be doing?

What do you do in your leisure time?

What kind of learning activities are you a part of?

Let images wander freely into your mind and the feelings they bring flow into your heart. How do each of your life areas complement the others? Which area needs more time and attention now?

Your heart and mind are now filled with comfort and joy. And know in your heart of hearts that you can conjure this vision whenever you need reminding of what is important to you. Know that holding this life vision close to your heart will help you to manifest it in reality.

Smart Tip
➡ Create images or pictures to help you visualize your life vision. Or develop a logo that represents your life.

Guidelines For Writing Your Life Vision
1. Meditate about what you would like your life to look like and be like.
2. Jot down any thoughts, feelings, or images that came up during your meditation.
3. Sketch out a picture or symbol of something important to your life vision.
4. Write a rough draft.
5. Write your life vision statement, in present terms, as if it is already that way.
6. Keep it to one page.

7. Include statements from the four main life areas: love, labor, leisure, and learning.
8. Include your top three values.

You will know you have finished with your life vision when you feel at peace with it.

Smart Tip

➡ Don't worry about how you are going to create and live out your life vision.
   Simply get it down on paper. The "How" will come later, for no focus on the "Why."

Sample Life Vision

In this life, I play a dual role of *student and teacher.* I am a collector and imparter of wisdom to all who surround me. As a spiritual being having a human experience, I learn my soul's lessons so that I will evolve.

I know that life is a gift to be unwrapped daily and that there are four main spheres of human experience: *love, labor, leisure, and learning.*

In love,   I practice patience and empathy with others.
            I am a positive role model for my family, friends,
            colleagues, and students.
            I seek out real connections with other
            like-minded souls.
            I bestow loving words and kind gestures
            onto those closest to me.

In labor,   I educate and empower others to make conscious,
            smart decisions.
            I help others follow their intuition and trust
            themselves.
            I openly express myself through the spoken
            and written word.
            I am creative and unique in my approach to work.

In leisure,   I honor my mind, body and spirit.
I take time to relax, rejuvenate and have fun.
I actively participate in healthy activities.
I connect with nature and animals as a
source of inspiration.

In learning,   I take risks and do not fear failure; rather,
I see mistakes as
learning opportunities.
I am a lifelong learner.
I overcome obstacles, believe in myself and
achieve my goals.
When confused, I look to my higher self for guidance.

I consciously and intentionally create my life
around my core values:
Abundance (emotional, financial, and spiritual).
Balance (in my personal and professional spheres).
Contribution (making a difference in the world).

I operate from Acceptance, Authenticity, and Communication. I am willing to receive and appreciate the beauty, love, and wisdom available to me from nature and other human beings while on my journey.

When my Spirit takes flight, I will look upon my life with happiness, joy, and inner peace—knowing that my existence on earth held meaning for myself and others.

Life Purpose Statement

To uncover your life's work, you must get clear on what you want by practicing visualization, knowing your purpose, and then living it out by the powerful act of creation. Once you know what vision you have for your life, you can move on to developing your purpose statement. When your work seems more like play, you are working on purpose. The thing about a purpose is that you may find yourself engaging in it both in and out of work. You can't separate your purpose from who you are, so you will find that it often flows into your personal life.

A purpose statement is a broad-based declaration of what you feel passionate about providing to the world and/or what you want to share with others in terms of your life's work. It is not a career objective or limited to a job title or career field. Keep it to a sentence in length and phrase it so that it clearly communicates to others what you want to accomplish via your life's work.

For example, **my life purpose is to educate and empower people to make smarter decisions in important life areas.**

Sample words for your Purpose Statement:

Advance	Advise	Affirm	Choose
Coordinate	Compose	Counsel	Create
Demonstrate	Develop	Educate	Encourage
Express	Facilitate	Give	Heal
Inspire	Invent	Involve	Lead
Love	Make	Motivate	Organize
Perform	Promote	Raise	Support
Strive	Teach	Touch	Validate
Value	Wisdom	Write	

Smart Tip

➡ Post your life vision and life purpose statements in your office, so you can reflect on them daily.

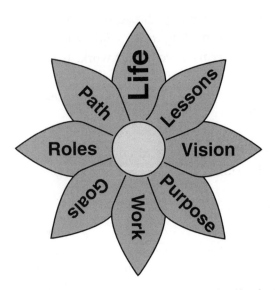

The most fulfilling life is one where you individually design and tailor it to your specifications.

Your *life* is like a big, beautiful blooming flower with numerous uniquely decorated petals making up your unique experience:

Your *lessons* are your personal learning and growth opportunities.

Your *vision* is an overall blueprint for the kind of life you want to lead.

Your *purpose* is what you want to share with others.

Your *life's work* are the on-going personal and professional projects you complete.

Your *goals* are mini-steps that help to support your work, purpose, and vision.

Your *roles* are the parts that you play along your journey.

Your *path* is the way you choose to create your life by the conscious choices you make during your journey.

You must find your path and bravely follow it wherever it leads.

Journal Assignment #8
Write your life vision and life purpose statements.

Chapter Six

Work in the 21st Century

*"Your success in life does not altogether depend on ability and training.
It also depends on your determination to grasp opportunities
that are presented to you."*
—Paramahansa Yogananda

What is Work?

Work is the use of energy, skills or personal resources to bring about desired results in an undertaking, enterprise, endeavor, or job. Despite what our culture tends to preach *all work* can be meaningful, if you approach it with the right attitude (with love and respect for others). Some people may feel that they have wasted time in unrewarding work-related tasks. It does not have to be that way, if you can find the meaning that position may hold for you. Often, when we have a job we don't particularly like, we become depressed. Many people think it is "beneath" them to perform the menial tasks in life. But all work is valuable, and in order to find meaning in your work, you must first find the lesson. Perhaps you were meant to have that experience, so that you could learn something else—a skill or personal quality that will be helpful to you in the future.

Buddha said, *"Right livelihood is work done consciously with pure intent and service."* The work that is performed is a direct reflection of society's standards and values, which gets filtered down to the individual—we do the work that is available, which is the work that is viewed as important. For instance, we used to think that manufacturing products was a priority. Now we think servicing customers is a priority. As society's mores and values become more complex and differentiated, people are deciding for themselves what work needs to be done and then creating their own opportunities. I think it is safe to say that work in the 21st century is in the process of reinvention. For example, for a long time "society" did not think conserving and preserving our natural resources was important, but now tens of thousands of people have created their life's work based on environmental issues.

In the Industrial Age, the richest person in the world owned natural resources. In the Information Age, the richest person in the world owns information/knowledge. And the business of retrieving, storing, and disseminating information is what our high-tech, cyber world is all about. From the farms to the factories, work meant long hours and hard labor in exchange for the feeling of a job well done and a paycheck. Today, people are getting very rich who have put in very little (if any) blood, sweat, or tears into their daily work. Thanks (or no thanks) to the Internet, companies are going public at the blink of an eye and twenty-one-year olds are becoming instant millionaires. Obviously, this new worker has put to rest the old idea of "working hard pays off."

Now more than ever, *what is work?* is an interesting question because all of our ideas about what is important and how to "make it" in the world of work are changing. Our ideas about how one should earn a living are changing. In the "good ole days," it took a long time to earn a fortune. Nowadays, we live in a get rich quick world, where people spend millions upon millions of dollars on lottery tickets and who hope to get on game shows that feature everyday, ordinary people becoming instant millionaires.

What is Your Concept of Work?

Defining what your concept of work is will enable you to *create* your life's work. Stop and think about the who, what, where, when and why do you want to work? And try to consider what would be a healthy fit for you? Be sure to consider your life vision and life purpose statements when you answer these questions.

Who do you want to work with?
Children, teenagers, adults? Upper, middle, or lower class? Similar or different background?
What kind of work do you want to do?
Self Employed: Work at home or at an office? Travel?

Organization Employed: Small, medium, large? Corporate? Non-profit?

Project-Employed: Free-lance? Contractor? Consultant?

Where do you want to work?

Inside or outside? For a small company or Fortune 500? In a big city or small town?

When do you want to work?

Day or night? Full-time, part-time, or temporary? Year round or seasonal?

Why do you want to work?

For the challenge? Money/benefits? Opportunity to share your gifts?

Of course keep in mind your overall lifestyle. How much money do you need to earn in order to live the kind of life you want? The smart thing to do is to live within your means and create a career that allows you to have the time to enjoy other things in life.

What Most People Need From Work

- A sense of meaning in the work they perform
- Appropriate challenge and stimulation
- A work environment that adds to their overall life happiness and balance between autonomy and support
- The opportunity to apply their ksa's (knowledge, skills, and abilities)
- Appropriate feedback and recognition (either from a supervisor or customers)
- Fair pay, benefits/perks
- Enjoyable work activities
- Professional development opportunities

Do You Work to Live or Live to Work?

What kind of worker are you? Someone who has a balance between working and living? Or are you a workaholic? As spiritual beings, we are meant to seek happiness. Fulfillment comes from many sources, work is simply one of them. Is it important not to let society's standards of the 50-60 hour work week dictate how you work.

As a society, we need to learn to relax. All work and no play is making us dull. Due to overwork and more time constraints, we are not fully living or working at our peak potential. How is it that Americans barely get two weeks of vacation a year and Europeans enjoy a month of "holiday" every year? In fact, we have been taught to be rugged individualists, fiercely independent people who have to fight for everything we get. We want to direct our destiny and be the master of our domain, which can be helpful in most cases. But when we go against nature, we go against ourselves. When it comes to modern career development, I advocate "becoming," which is a lifelong process of following your intuition and keeping your skills updated as the best way to stay employed. But most career development programs and counselors focus on what "job" or "title" you want to hold. Just look at the pressure we put on children to be productive, and to make major decisions and choices. It is somewhat frightening that as early as nine or ten, we are asking what little Johnny wants to be when he grows up. Some of the most interesting people I have met who are in their 50's and 60's still haven't figured that one out!

College is another place where career plans and expectations are forced on young people. Having worked with college students for several years, I cannot tell you how many of them choose majors and careers because of parental pressure, rather than basing it on what felt right to them. What is going on here? Does it really matter if you don't know exactly what you want to do in the world of work while you are still in school? College is a time for exploration and discovery, not limiting, premature career/life decisions. The fact is most people will not be staying in the same job they had when they first got out of college. But if they haven't learned how to *become,* then they will continue to believe they have to choose one thing.

Sad to say, grownups don't get much of a break either. Adult students who return to school to finish a degree, seldom return because they want to know more about the world or themselves, or to learn for the sake of learning, but rather to get "a better job." The mindset here is that a better job leads to a better life, which may or may not be true. Believe it or not, it is *o.k.* not to have everything figured out about life! The best we can do is to stay centered in who we are and what we have to offer, and feel positive about the uncertainty of life. We put too much pressure on ourselves to know exactly what we want and how to get it—to have all the answers. What we should be cultivating in our children is a different focus. Instead of concentrating on *what* they want to be, or what we want them to be, let's focus on helping them realize *who* they want to become.

The question really comes down to not the "how" of work, but the "why?" There are two main applications.

The Practicality of Work (Human Application)

When Humans are @Work, we work:

To provide service to others
To provide sufficient financial support to live our lives comfortably
To create products and services for our consumption

Because the world is changing and we are experiencing shifts in demographics and economics, and becoming a more global society with an emphasis on technology—we have to consciously decide what kind of world we want to leave to our grandchildren.

People who work with half a heart and/or only for the end result (the paycheck) are not only doing a disservice to themselves, but to others as well.

The Spirituality of Work (Soul Application)

When our Spirit is @Work, we work:

To express our soul
To elevate the state of society, so we can enjoy the fruits of our labors
To move us forward on our path towards enlightenment

Where there is a large majority of underemployed people, it negatively impacts on society as a whole. Human beings need to feel they are giving and sharing with others in a meaningful way, which means all people have an inherent need to do some kind of work.

People who work with passion and presence are soulful workers. That is because they share their full selves with others, no matter what work they may be performing.

Soulful Work

Ralph Waldo Emerson once said, *"The one thing in the world of value, is the active soul."* In other words, a person who is actively living, working, and loving in this world is making a real contribution. How can we contribute to a better workplace? How can we bring more of our

Spirit to our work? By sharing more of our real selves with others, by being aware of what our purpose is, and by doing our work in a loving way. If part of our mission is to evolve to a higher level of awareness— of being—by learning important lessons, then we need to become more aware of the power of *choice*. Sometimes we may choose to learn our lessons the easy way, sometimes the hard way. In work, we have inevitably learned our lessons both ways. When we *consciously create* our life's work, our soul has the opportunity to learn more meaningful ways to express itself.

As enlightened beings, we will not confuse our job or titles with who we really are. We will know that our Spirit is meant to learn and experience many things, and that everything in life is temporary (even a bad job or situation). We will realize that Oliver Wendell Holmes was right when he said, *"Every calling is great, when greatly pursued."*

Buddha taught that the only reality is impermanence and change. And that it is best not to resist. (No wonder the Buddha looks so relaxed!) The way we choose to approach our life's work impacts on how fulfilled we feel, and our overall effect on others. The more we can bring our Spirit into our work, the more soulful the experience for all. When we care about the work we do, no matter how menial the task, we pay attention to the details and take pride in our craftsmanship.

Creating meaningful work springs from problems or issues that need to be solved or addressed. Many of which come from "socially responsible" contexts. Sunny Hansen, in her book *Integrative Life Planning,* offers several ideas for different areas that could use a helping hand:
Utilizing Technology Constructively, Preserving the Environment,
Understanding Family and Work Changes, Reducing Violence,
Advocating for Human Rights, Accepting Changing Gender Roles,
Valuing Human Diversity, Discovering New Ways of Knowing.

When you are doing your life's work, it will feel almost like play because it will so enjoyable and rewarding. It's as if your work is your hobby and your hobby is your work. When you are sharing your gifts and talents, time flies! Unlike when you have a job, the time drags, and you have to know exactly the "right" way to do something. Working on projects for your life's work keeps you wondering how and what to do next. In fact, you are not exactly sure where you are going with it, rather it evolves as you get further into it.

Your life's work, like your entire life, does not have a specific direction or map. It just shows up and you have to follow it. I know that when I am called to write, I simply must do it. I don't really know where I'm headed with it, but I'm not concerned. The next step in my process comes from my intuitive self, and I follow my inner guide. The "message" flows naturally and effortlessly as a result. When you are working on *purpose,* instead of going through the motions, the motions go through you. You flow with your work and your work flows through you. In fact, the work will show you how to do it. This quote from an unknown author sums up how you will surely feel when you are doing your life's work:

"A master in the art of living draws no sharp distinction between his work and play, his labor and his leisure, his mind and his body, his education and his recreation. He hardly knows which is which, he simply pursues his vision of excellence through whatever he is doing and leaves others to determine whether is working or playing. To himself, he always seems to be doing both."

The Modern World of Work

Since the modern world of work is rapidly changing to keep up with the demands of our fast-paced lives and lifestyles, here are some characteristics of what the new work contract will look like:

*   Seeking more meaning from work.
*   Equating "career success" with personal satisfaction over paycheck or status.
*   More self-employment, short-term and contractual work.
*   Everyone will need their own "name-brand."
*   Striving for life balance
*   Increased use of technology.
*   Finding work that needs doing.
*   Changing in the way management and leadership is conducted (less arrogance at the top level, more power on lower levels).
*   Increased need for networking and self-marketing.
*   Lifelong "trying on" of various roles, jobs, and industries.

- Lack of loyalty between employee and organization.
- Creating a plan that is flexible, and continually assessing the "fit" of the work.
- Increased representation of women and minorities in the workforce.
- Changing career fields numerous times in a lifetime.
- Self-responsibility: Everyone knowing they have to chart their own career direction.
- Dedication to quality customer service in all career fields.
- Emphasis on lifelong learning.

Advantages of the Modern World of Work

- More career opportunities for everyone!
- Freedom to choose from a variety of jobs, tasks, and assignments!
- More flexibility in how and where work is performed, i.e. working from home or telecommuting!
- More control over your own time!
- Greater opportunity to express yourself through your work!
- Ability to shape and reshape your life's work in accordance with your values and interests!
- Increased opportunity to develop other skills by working in various industries and environments!
- Self-empowerment mindset!
- Allows you to create situations or positions where you can fill a need in the world that is not being filled!
- Opportunity to present yourself as an independent contractor or vendor with services to offer!

Top Ten Skills For the New World of Work

1. Communication
The ability to effectively communicate your thoughts and ideas in person, on paper, and over the telephone. To listen to others and be open to other viewpoints and opinions.

2. Creativity

The ability to think and act "out of the box." To discover new and innovative ways of thinking and doing things.

3. Technology

The ability to understand and utilize computer systems, the latest software, etc. To use the computer in your daily life and on the job.

4. Team Work

The ability to work effectively in a team situation. To be able to utilize the right people to get the best results. To be willing to lead and to follow.

5. Flexibility

The ability to "go with the flow." To change on an as-needed basis. To become multi-task oriented, to be able to change hats frequently.

6. Information Management

The ability to know where to get needed information. To be able to search, locate, and retrieve information. To utilize various resources, whether they be people, printed materials, or the vast world of technology.

7. Self Management

The ability to manage oneself in personal and professional situations. To be able to respond appropriately to stressful situations.

8. Customer Care

The ability to care about the needs and concerns of other people, especially those you serve. To "go the extra mile" for your customers or clients.

9. Character

The ability to project a positive image by acting in a manner that reflects trust, confidence, honesty, and integrity.

10. Personal Development

The ability to continuously improve upon one's skill set. To be dedicated to lifelong learning.

Journal Assignment #9

Are you ready for the modern world of work? What skills do you possess that make you marketable? What skills can you develop?

Chapter Seven

Define Your Career, Create Your Life's Work

"Destiny is not a matter of chance, it is a matter of choice.
It is not a thing to be waited for, it is a thing to be achieved."
—Williams Jennings Bryan

What is a Career Anyway?

A career is the sum total of all of your work-related contributions to society in a lifetime. This includes time and effort spent to provide goods, services, or benefit to others. A career includes paid, un-paid, volunteer, part-time, and full-time positions. Your career includes many life roles you may not think of: student, homemaker, babysitter, office worker, doctor, lawyer, etc. A career encompasses all the roles you play and duties you perform. You may have many jobs or positions that make up your career, but you only have <u>one</u> overall career. There are various career options in the modern world of work: Self-Employed, Organization Employed, or Project-Employed.

By definition, career development is *the interaction of psychological, sociological, economic, physical and chance factors that shape the sequence of jobs, occupations, or positions a person may engage in throughout his or her lifetime.* Career development is an on-going process that includes the aspects of planning and strategizing your career based on information about your self, the world of work, the match between them, and the action you will take to create your life's work. Formal career development occurs in high schools, colleges and universities, adult education programs, business and industry, military, community and government agencies, trade and technical schools. Consider all the places you have developed your career with either academic or work experience. Where can you go next and what can you do to further develop your career?

You have the power to create what you want, whether you wish to be self-employed, change career fields entirely, hold a certain kind of position, or volunteer your time. Smart career development requires you to be self-reflective, resourceful, motivated, flexible, and able to keep your skills and competencies up-to-date.

Contemporary Career Concepts

Statistics say that we will experience many job transitions throughout our life. For example: the U.S. Department of Labor says that the average person will have 3.5 different careers in his lifetime and work for ten employers, keeping each job for 3.5 years.

From the 1995 National Association of Colleges and Employers *Journal of Career Planning*, "The average American beginning his or her career in the 1990s will probably work in ten or more jobs for five or more employers before retiring."

In the mid 1990s, Richard Knowdell said that "Career planning in the 1950s and 1960s was like riding on a train. The train remained on the track and one could quite possibly stay on that track until retirement day. In the 1970s and 1980s career planning was like getting on a bus. One could change buses and it was a little closer to driving than on a train. For the 1990s and beyond, career planning is more like an all-terrain vehicle. The worker gets to drive, has to read the map, and has to be attuned to the terrain, which could change from moment to moment."

When I attended a recent California Career Development Conference, I heard several other metaphors to describe the career development process: One person said, "The old career was a marriage. The new career is a date." And someone else mentioned, "a career was like going to an amusement park, where you go from one ride to the next."

Obviously, the concept of climbing the career ladder is antiquated. Rather than "moving up" in one organization, you will find yourself moving up, down, and even off the ladder. It could, in fact, seem more like a maze, with many twists and turns, stops and starts.

My own concept of career is like a wardrobe, where you "try on" different outfits throughout your lifetime, and continue to check the mirror to see if it still fits and matches your current style and taste. In the modern world of work, you will need to find work that is "suited" to you. Think of your life's work as your wardrobe. It is ever-changing as you move through life, changing as your styles and interests change. Throughout the process, you will be tailoring yourself to fit different roles, and to meet changing work styles and expectations.

Thus, today, the way in which we go about planning and strategizing our work life is constantly changing. We are taking a more proactive, therefore more exciting and challenging approach— to managing which way our career takes us. People are daring to walk their unique paths, and ignoring traditional routes. In fact, tomorrow's jobs are relatively unknown to us at this time, as there will be new titles and new career fields that will develop. If a modern career is like a wardrobe, you will wear many kinds of outfits throughout a lifetime, sometimes mixing and matching assemblies, but always checking to see that it still matches your current style and remains a good fit. It has been said that clothes make the man—what you are displaying to the world through your choice of clothing is how you express yourself. Similarly, how you express yourself and what you value is reflected in the work you choose to perform.

As Mark Twain said, *"There is no security in life, only opportunity."* Given today's changing times, we cannot hold onto one idea for very long—there is so much good work that must be done to help us evolve to our fullest potential. We are multi-talented, multi-faceted beings with many gifts to share. We cannot lock ourselves into any one job or job path. We must walk our path, but remain flexible and open to new experiences. We also need to learn our lessons along the way, as each job, no matter how small is meaningful and is part of our career plan, in that we are always building onto our careers. Today's work will prepare us for tomorrow's opportunities.

Is a Career a Calling or Choice?

How much of our career path is destiny and how much is free will? In my opinion, it is 50/50. We are given a life map at the beginning of our lives, and there are things we are meant to learn, people we are meant to meet, work we are meant to perform. But many of us are not tuned into ourselves and the signs that are presented to us. We often miss important information, and miss out on those lessons, people, and jobs.

The use of *free will* comes about when we are presented with options. Choices are really curves in our path. We can choose to take the long route, or the quicker, easier route. No path is better, it just impacts how quickly we move along our route, but remember: when climbing the mountain of self discovery, taking the long, hard, scenic route can be a rather enjoyable, enlightening experience.

Confucius once said, *"Choose a career you love and you will never work another day in your life."* If you think about this, what a different experience we could have in our work lives. If we actually loved the work we were doing, it wouldn't seem so much like our traditional concept of work (drudgery/pain). Think about it! How many jobs have you had that you dreaded going to? What are some of the differences between a job, a career, and your life's work? Let's define it.

A **job** is something you get paid to do (money is the primary motivation). It is easy to perform because there is not much challenge, and you will eventually find other work to do.

It may or may not fully engage you. Spirit may or may not be present.

A **career** is something you get paid to do that is viewed as a profession (status or identity is the motivation). It may provide more challenge, but after a while, you may get burned out, and choose to stop doing it.

It may or may not fully engage you. Spirit may or may not be present.

Your **life's work** is something you do whether you get paid for it or not (your soul's need for expression is the motivation). There is plenty of challenge and personal meaning. You will always want to do it.

It definitely fully engages you. Spirit is present.

Remember that a job can get you started toward your life's work. In fact, jobs provide the very important element of *exposure* to different kinds of industries. Take for example, a woman who started out working in a department store as a clerk, who moved into a management position, and finally created her life's work as an independent contractor who trains others in customer service skills.

Get Smart!

➡ If everyone in the world could create their life's work (and they can!)—if everyone could find what they were meant to do in life, how much happier and fulfilled we all would be!

Creating Your Life's Work
Life Vision + Life Purpose + Action= Your Life's Work

The *Get Smart!* formula for creating your life's work:
Combine your life vision (the overall vision for the four dimensions of your life) with your life purpose (how you choose to share your gifts with others) with action (conscious intention and attention) to equal your life's work (the personal and professional projects you complete in a lifetime).

Laurence G. Boldt in his book *Zen and the Art of Making a Living,* discusses how your life's work is a mixture of *Integrity* (living in alignment with your values, doing work that you can be proud of, and having a sense of purpose), *Service* (making the world a better place to live, giving back to others, and feeling as if your work makes a significant contribution), *Enjoyment* (loving what you do, doing work that allows you to fully express your talents, and creating new ideas or things), and *Excellence* (giving your all to something, dedicating yourself to quality, and having a sense of pride in your work). Looking at your life's work using these models should help you to choose a career based on what you want to *do*, not on who you want to be. For instance, wanting to perform work that helps others lead healthier lives provides several options—doctor, nurse, scientist, health educator. However, if you narrowly focus on being a doctor, you may miss other valuable work-related, meaningful opportunities. This mindset also naturally opens you up to playing many different kinds of roles, while continuing to stay on purpose.

If you remember that humanity's mission is to learn to love, and know that your individual purpose is to do the work you were meant to do, you are well on your way. Now, you must take action. *"Find your real job and do it,"* as Charlotte Perkins Gilman said over a half century ago. We can find meaning in all of the work that we do, but there is still something special that must be done by each one of us. Our life's work, then, is to continually find work that allows us to fully express our gifts, talents, and knowledge in order to positively impact our world. Once you find out what your life's work is, you will have to make some changes. For example, you discover that you are meant to design clothes for petite women. You think, *"Great! I finally know what I am meant to do!"* And then you think, *"Not great! I don't know much about designing clothes!"* Now, your commitment comes in, because you may have to go back to school to learn the elements of fashion design and marketing. You may have to leave a well-paying (albeit boring job) to pursue your dream. I never said it would be easy, did I?

Some people think that work is all about pleasure and fun. Others think it is toil and pain. The fact is that work is a little of both, at one time or another. When you are disillusioned with life or your work you will tend to continually compare yourself to others and their work will always look better than your work. But remember that everyone has different time-lines to start the process of creating their true life's work. Some know what they are meant to do at an early age, while others need half a lifetime to figure it out. You are where you are meant to be for the moment. Just keep your vision in mind, and focus on the work at hand while creating ways to manifest your life purpose.

The Joy of Service

No matter what work we are doing, we can accomplish more of both our universal and individual purposes by performing work that involves service to others. Ego concerns itself with titles and salary amounts. Spirit concerns itself with the work that helps others, that works in a loving way. To the spirit, all work that is done in loving fashion has worth. When we are unawakened, we continue to follow the path of ego. But as we wake up to who we really are, we will realize that work in just a function of our Spirit, and that it serves a soulful purpose.

Your life's work is made up of the services you provide to others. It includes what you do for financial reward, as well as what you do for psychological reward. To create the work you were meant to do, you must first have mental creation, then physical creation. Owning up to your personal power and life purpose is no easy task. It requires that you make a conscious choice to say *yes, I will do this*. When you go about creating your life's work, you can't be a wimp! You must be strong and believe that you can succeed. Your life's work will interweave your values, knowledge, interests, skills, and combine it with inner contentment and outer challenge.

When you are making smart career choices, you are using your internal wisdom and external information. How much thought, energy, and time do you put into your major life decisions? Do you just let life happen to you? Or do you create your life based on your vision? When you are in the starring role of your life— directing it and managing it—you will gain a sense of empowerment that will help you to make smarter choices in other life areas. When you are empowered, you may scare yourself and others. Even those closest to you may resent you for making these changes. They will outwardly say "congratulations" but inwardly will be thinking *"who does she think she is?"* She doesn't deserve to have opened her own business, been promoted, landed that job, or whatever.

Until you start *believing* in abundance, many negative energies will be lying in wait for you once you start on your true path. You may be surprised to find that others will put obstacles in your way just to trip you up. This will likely be the result of their envy and resentment because they have not mustered the courage to take charge of their own lives. No matter what, don't believe what "they" say. You are worthy and deserving of experiencing the kind of life and doing the kind of work you have always wanted to do. Just stay true to yourself and ignore the naysayers. They will come around sooner or later. (And you may be able to help them achieve their dreams.) You are here on earth to help and serve, you just need to uncover your unique gifts and then share them with others.

Checklist for Your Life's Work

Put a check by each statement that is true regarding to the work that you do.

_____Strives for excellence and quality

_____Is personally satisfying and fulfilling

_____Gives meaning to your life
_____Allows you to express your unique purpose
_____Contains room for growth and development
_____Provides an appropriate amount of challenge and variety
_____Has been personally created by you
_____Requires a healthy amount of energy, but is not too draining
_____Feels like a natural fit for your gifts and talents
_____Is work that is in tune with your nature
_____Provides something useful or beautiful for the world
_____Is something you would do even if no one paid you for it
_____Is a reflection of what you value
_____Enables you to express your inner self
_____You do not have everything figured out about your work, but are able to follow the work where it leads you

Are You Ready For Your Career Search Process?

Respond to each statement by selecting which number represents your level of comfort.

1: Strongly Agree
2: Agree
3: Maybe, not certain
4: Disagree
5: Strongly Agree

Self-Awareness

I can identify and articulate my knowledge, skills, and abilities.   ____
I know what I like and dislike about different work situations.   ____
I have a general idea of how I see my career developing over the next 5-10 years.   ____
I am aware of my personal strengths and weaknesses.   ____

Attitude

I have a positive and optimistic view of my career future.   ____
I am confident that I have the knowledge, skills,

and abilities that can be of use and interest to
potential employers or customers.   ____
I enjoy working.   ____
My work is a reflection of what I deem important.   ____

Networking

I can identify and target employers and customers
that would be interested in my skills.   ____
I have an extensive work referral network.   ____
I feel comfortable talking with people about
my skills and abilities.   ____
I am involved in professional associations
and groups on a regular basis.   ____

Knowledge of the World of Work

I know the fields that are growing in the
world of work.   ____
I know which jobs are compatible with my
education and experience.   ____
I expect to work in various career fields
in my lifetime.   ____
I know where to go to get career information
and job leads.   ____

Technology Know-How

I have well-developed computer skills.   ____
I can utilize at least 10 on-line job posting sites
that relate to my field of interest.   ____
I have a well-designed website.   ____
I can use the Internet to research and
find needed information.   ____

Career Search Skills

I can clearly explain and provide examples of what
I know about and can do.   ____
My resume and cover letters are targeted,
well-written, and error free.   ____
I can write different types of effective career

correspondence: cover letters, thank-you letters,
brochures, etc.   ____
I can negotiate a salary 5-15% above what
someone initially offers me.   ____
I am able to adapt to the changing needs of the
market by keeping my skills up to date.   ____
I can provide excellent references or testimonials
regarding the quality of my work.   ____
I have a well-developed brand name.   ____
I believe in lifelong learning.   ____

Get Smart!
➡ The lower the score, the more ready you are for the career search
process. The higher the score, the less ready you are for the career
search process.

28-48 is excellent.
49-59 is good
60-75 is fair
76-101 is poor
102 or over: you may want to consult a career coach to help you get
ready for the search.

Journal Assignment #10
To find more about what your life's work might be, answer these questions: If you could provide one thing for the world, what it would be
and why? What are you doing when time passes by without your realizing it? What do you think are some of the important issues in today's
world? How can you be of service to others?

Chapter Eight

The Return of the Entrepreneur

"If I reach for the sun, I may hit a star."
—PT Barnum

Be an Entrepreneur

A recent Internet poll of 25-44 year olds, revealed that 90% of them hoped to own their own business. A survey conducted by Ernst & Young found that 75% of influential Americans believe that entrepreneurship will be the defining trend of the 21st century. Some of the factors that have attributed to the rise of the modern day entrepreneurial spirit is access to technology, a global economy, and corporate stagnation. Many workers have experienced feelings of discontent, which is likely due to the upsizing, downsizing, and right-sizing of corporations. But whatever the reason, modern workers want to have more control over the work they do. And they want work that is meaningful and important to them. *Now is a great time to become your own boss.* In fact, the number of Americans who are running their own businesses will continue to grow as we move further into the millenium. As workers values are changing and people want more time to do the things they love with those they love, having employment that allows for a greater balance in their lives is critical to today's worker.

In fact, it is downright un-American not to believe in the principles of entrepreneurship. We started out working on the family farm or in the family-owned grocery store (or other small business), but as our country became more industrialized, families were pulled apart. We had to go where the work was. We left our homes and hometowns and ventured into the big cities. Big companies, industries, and corporations popped up all over the country, and we became reliant on them to take care of us. Today, with the advent of the computer, we don't even have to leave home to conduct business. It frees us up to concentrate on the "business of life" again.

And we are also returning to the concept of performing more work for the community. Back in the early 20th century, we had a strong sense of self-reliance and family ties. Matthew Fox talks about this in his book *The Reinvention of Work*: "*Life and livelihood ought not be separated but to flow from the same source, which is the spirit...spirit means life, and both life and livelihood are about living in depth, living with meaning, purpose, joy, and a sense of contributing to the greater community.*"

The new world of work encourages the entrepreneurial mindset, in that we need to learn to use our imagination to dream up new ideas, challenge assumptions and belief systems to find a better way, and break through worn-out thinking to create new and innovative products and services. This way of thinking is helpful whether you are working for yourself or someone else. An entrepreneur can be defined as *anyone who undertakes a commercial risk for profit, and/or tackles new challenges.* They are the change agents of society because they see a problem and want to find a way to solve it. They believe in being self-reliant and taking action to better their communities. Robert Schwartz's definition: *"An entrepreneur is essentially a visualizer and actualizer. He can visualize something and when he visualizes it, he sees exactly how to make it happen."* Successful entrepreneurs realize that if it is to become a reality, they are the ones to make it be. An entrepreneur is someone who is able to continually reinvent himself, and to rethink an entire project (and possibly start all over) if he finds that something is not right. Thus, someone who has vision, flexibility, and a risk-taking nature fares very well in self-employment ventures.

Of course, like anything else, there are pros and cons to becoming an entrepreneur. One pro is that you are the boss. The con is that you still have other co-workers, customers, and vendors to rely on to get the job done. People who are self-employed often only have illusions of control. For instance, you may think you have everything under control and then something happens that puts everything out of your control. The difference is that being the boss means that it all comes down to you. You are fully responsible for your success. For many people this level of personal responsibility is part of the challenge and enjoyment. The truth is that any successful entrepreneur rolls with the punches and moves with the winds of change. This quote from an unknown author sums up what is takes to be an entrepreneur:

"Excellence can be attained if you care more than others think is wise.

Risk more than others think is sage.

Dream more than others think is practical.

Expect more than others think is possible."

Stubbornness and Boldness are Strengths

When it comes to following your heart and creating work that matters, be stubborn. That's right. For far too long, stubborn people have been given a bad rap. Always stand up for what you believe to be right when you are creating your life's work. Why? Because along the way, people and obstacles will try to prevent you from achieving what you want. You can't give up at the first one, two, or ten rejections to your idea. In fact, you must persevere and keep at it. You must stubbornly hold onto your dreams.

Two things can help you to become a stubborn, bold entrepreneur: humility and self confidence. Since you are bound to come up against some rough times, humility can help you learn your lessons and move on. Having a healthy ego, one that is big enough to allow you to feel good about yourself, but not too big that you fail to see the big picture, can help with your self confidence. Self confidence goes hand-in-hand with humility, in that you will continue to "get up to bat" even after you have struck out a few times.

However, do not be so stubborn that you fail to see when a new direction needs to be taken or new strategy implemented. You still may have the right idea, but may be going about it the wrong way. That is when you need to be stubborn about succeeding, but open to other ways for your work to manifest itself. Sometimes, you only need to re-design (make some improvements) and other times you may need to re-direct (take another route). If you are following your intuitive guidance, you will receive the messages in order to make smart decisions.

If you want to work for yourself, recognize your gifts, fully embrace them, and surrender yourself to creativity. Genius is brash and bold—it smashes convention, refuses to be ignored, and makes its own rules. Boldness has raw tenacity and a need to show its power and roughness. There is nothing wrong with that, especially when you are going after something as important as your career. Bold people dive into their work with gusto and bravery, they give 110% because they love what they do! Nothing is done halfway.

Bold people think *big*. They want to do things that have never been done before. Thank goodness for those people! Without them, we probably wouldn't have electricity, telephones, cars, or personal computers. In truth, all great inventions, all history-changing break-throughs—and many of the best things in life are a direct result of someone who thought big. Initially, though, everyone will say "that will never work." Like Louis Dembitz Brandeis said, *"Most of the things worth doing in the world had been declared impossible before they were done."*

What mission impossible will you make possible? How big do you dare dream? What are you willing to try even if it might fail? You could want to be the next person on Mars, or perhaps to simply lead a healthy and happy life with your family. Either way, you have got to *want* it badly enough to survive the critics and naysayers, who will ask "Who do you think you are?"

A bold person intimidates other people. Get used to it. They wish they could do what you are doing. After all, you are the person who dares think it and dares do it. You are worthy of achieving your dreams. You are good enough, smart enough, and brave enough. When you are gutsy, you take the unconventional route, and may have to say and do unpopular things, even to those closest to you. But when you are living at your maximum potential, there is no more "I should have's" or "If only's." You are not just dreaming about it, you are doing it!

I will say that bold men can get away with their brashness more than women. Bold women sometimes get labeled "bitch." But do not let that stop you, ladies. Bold people rarely let what other people think about them prevent them from creating what they want from life. And, for the first time, statistics show that more women are starting small businesses than men.

You must also be a strong person in the face of fear and failure. Don't let fear of failure or rejection hinder you. Most people give up too soon after only the first one or two attempts. You must persist if you want to see real results. Stubborn, bold people perceive failure as a learning opportunity. Look at our 16th President, Abraham Lincoln.

He had two failed businesses, two bankruptcies, and was defeated in over six elections in his lifetime. He was not afraid of failure and never gave up on his dream of becoming President of the United States.

Obviously not everyone is born self-confident, but the good news is that you can build your confidence. By tackling smaller things and experiencing success, you can move on to accomplish bigger things.

Are You the Entrepreneurial Type?

If you really think you have those entrepreneurial genes, and you hunger to be your own boss, below are some characteristics of a person well-suited for self-employment. See if you are one of them.

Check if applicable to you.
_____Responsible
_____Hard Worker
_____Risk Taker
_____Creative
_____Flexible
_____Follows through with ideas
_____Personable
_____Optimistic
_____Perceptive
_____Self-confident
_____Determined
_____High degree of energy
_____Innovative
_____Independent
_____Ability to anticipate needs
_____Effective communicator
_____Responsive to criticism
_____Able to take the lead
_____Learn from mistakes
_____Self-directed

Get Smart!
➡ How many did you check off? The more, the better, if you want to go into business for yourself.

Would you say that you are always, sometimes, or never like these statements:

1. I am goal and action-oriented.
2. I am a self-starter.
3. I am self-confident.
4. I am a persistent person.
5. I like taking risks.
6. I am flexible and adaptable when necessary.
7. I am a problem-solver.
8. I am an innovative thinker.
9. I can sell myself and/or my product to others.
10. I accept responsibility for my actions.
11. I enjoy networking.
12. I can function in an environment of uncertainty.
13. I like being in charge.
14. I am willing to devote whatever time and energy it takes to be successful.
15. I am able to see what needs to be done and then do it.

➡ **Get Smart!**

If you answered always to ten or more questions, you are probably the entrepreneurial type. If you answered sometimes or never to ten or more, you may be better off working for an organization.

Case Illustration

From a very young age, Philip had entrepreneurial talents. At fourteen he worked at the local pizza parlor, in his hometown of Cleveland, Ohio. He worked his way up to manager by the time he left to go to college. He then worked his way through college by doing all kinds of gardening and yard work for many of the professors. His part-time gig paid for his tuition, living expenses, and pepperoni pizza habit. When he graduated with his degree in business administration, he was recruited by a large restaurant chain for their management trainee program. With his degree and previous experience, he was a perfect fit. He became the manager of one of the chain's restaurants in Florida. After four years in the job, he realized that what he really wanted was to own his own restaurant.

Having an active leisure life was important to him—he loved liv-

ing near the beach— so he began researching local restaurant business opportunities. His love for pizza led him to a local chain with five franchise locations. He applied for and received a small business loan and bought all five restaurants. He now spends his time over-seeing the operations of each of his restaurants, eating pizza, and spending time at the beach.

Journal Assignment #11

We often forget how entrepreneurial we have been. Think back over your life. When did you play the role of entrepreneur? Was it recently? Maybe it was in college when you typed other students' papers for money or when you started a business on-the side. Maybe it was in high school when you sold the most t-shirts, or even as a child when you sold Girl Scout cookies. Write about all of your entrepreneurial experiences.

Self-Employment Terms

There are many different ways to be self-employed. Knowing the lingo can help you to know what your options are.

C Corporation: This kind of incorporation is used by many major companies, so that they can sell shares of stock to the public.
- Limited Liability
- Annual Registration
- Paper Intensive
- It does not have restrictions on the number of shareholders.

DBA: "Doing Business As" is when you work as a sole proprietor and the name of your business is different than your name. For example: Mary Smith starts a company named "Mary Smith & Associates," therefore she would have to file a form to operate with that business name.

Subchapter S Corporation: A company that has a limited number of shareholders and the profits are passed directly to the owner.
- Limited Liability
- Same as corporation

- No more than 75 owners/one class stock

Limited Liability Company: (Often referred to as LLC). This is similar to an "S Corporation," but has fewer disadvantages.
- Limited Liability
- Members draft operating agreement
- No limit on number/types of members.

Limited Partnership: This is a special partnership where one partner invests money, but does not participate in the daily activities of the business.

Partnership: You form a business partnership with one or more people. Debts and assets of the business are legally linked. Responsibilities are typically shared between partners.
- Unlimited Liability
- Dissolution
- Partnership agreement

Sole-proprietorship: You are personally responsible for all the business obligations and transactions.
- Unlimited Liability
- Easy formation
- One owner

Self-Employment Titles

Free Agent: This term is borrowed from the sports world, and defines a person who is free to go where ever they choose. She is not tied to one company or one job title. She is loyal to herself, to the work that she does, and to the companies that hire her.

Freelancer: Someone who works for several different companies at once, and on specific projects. He typically gets paid a set rate, but does not receive company benefits such as sick pay or vacation leave. Artists and writers have been common freelancers in the past, although many other people have begun "freelancing" in different career fields.

Independent Contractor: Someone who works for a company, but the company is not their employer. An independent contractor has the freedom to decide where, when, and how to get the work done that has been contracted for. He may be paid by the hour or by the project. Trainers and information specialists have been common independent contractors in the past, although many other people have begun "contracting" in different career fields.

Private Practice: Someone who has a professional practice. She may work from home, have an office, or travel. People in private practice usually hold professional credentials, i.e., lawyer, therapist, doctor.

Small Business Owner: Someone who is the owner of a small business. This could be run out of one's home, from an office, or via the Internet. There may be or may not be employees.

Smart Tip
➡ To save time and money, start your business on-the-side and build it up until you can make it your full time career.

Get Smart!
➡ Social trends are impacting how work is delivered. More than ever before, there are part-time, flexi-time, and job-sharing situations occurring within organizations. Thus, freeing more people to "moonlight" or start a business on the side. The time is ripe for self-employment!

Questions to Consider Before Starting Your Business

1. What can I do that combines my interests, abilities and skills to fill a market need?
2. How much money do I need to get my business started and keep it going for at least six months to one year?
3. Will I be offering a product or service that people will want to buy?
4. Have I done enough research on my idea to know that it is feasible?
5. Where can I perform my work? (At home, from an office, or on the road?)

6.   Should I be a sole proprietor, partner with someone,
      or become a corporation?
7.   How can I make my business distinct and different
      from my competitors?
8.   Who will I need to consult with to get the right information?
      (accountants, attorneys, bankers, insurance agents,
      marketing consultants).
9.   Can I handle the various aspects of running a business,
      such as product/service development, marketing,
      accounting, management, etc?
10.   When should I go full-time?

If money is an issue, be smart and start your business on a part-time basis. Give yourself time to plant the seeds of success, while having the security of a regular pay check. This makes sense financially in more ways than one, in that many banks will more readily grant loans to people who still have a steady income. By easing into your business, you can take some pressure off up-front, which is usually the toughest time. Once you see that it is doing well, you can quit and make your business your full-time job.

Get Branded

La Fontaine once said, *"By the work, one knows the workman."* He must have known long ago about the importance of branding. In today's competitive marketplace, establishing and maintaining a brand name is essential to your career success. A service or trade mark tells people immediately what you do. People will return to those companies or individuals who have an established brand that provides value and on whom they can trust.

In addition to having a brand name, you must develop a strategy to promote it to a targeted audience. The most important element to branding is having a strong sense of self and a clear vision. Your brand is your reputation and also what you are "known for." A brand is both an intellectual and emotional shorthand that communicates an indelible impression. Think of the more successful brand names and how easily their messages come to mind: Coca Cola: "The Real Thing." Ford Motor Company: "Like a Rock." Obviously, you may not reach the audience that these major corporations have, but when your name or company is mentioned, it should create an immediate positive impression for those people who are *your customers or coworkers.*

That is the power you are going for: *instant name recognition from your customers/clients.* You do not want them to have to figure out who you are and what you do—you want them to know it instantly by your "branding." The amazing thing is once you build a brand name, you will no longer need to struggle to find work; in fact, your work will find you.

How do you create a brand? First, you must know who you really are (at the soul level). Second, you must know what you want to become. Experts agree that it takes time—sometimes several years, to develop a brand. It also takes time and energy. To get the process started, you first need to determine what your present message is. *You can ask people what five words come to mind when you think of me? What I do best? What do you think I stand for personally/professionally?*

Gather your information and see if it fits with what you are trying to communicate to your customers. If not, make some strategic plans to change your message. Think about what you would like to be known for, if you are not known for it already.

You should also develop an "elevator statement," which is a simple two-minute response to the question that many people ask: "What do you do?"

I am a_____

Who does_____

For_____

They choose me because of_____.

Once you have an idea of your message, ask yourself:

Is it simple?

Does it come naturally and easily?

Is the statement believable?

Does it matter if someone believes you?

Smart Tip

➡   All answers should be "yes."

Brand You

In addition to the development of your message, you need to become an expert and have a personal style that stands out from others in your field. What if you are an independent contractor or consultant? How can you develop an effective *Brand Me*? To do that you have to be extremely focused on what you do that adds value (you cannot be all things to all people), and find ways to actively promote yourself.

Remember that everything you do, from giving a formal presentation to answering the telephone sends a message. How you conduct your business will either reinforce your brand or diffuse it. You want to be sure that what you are offering has substance, but that you also put your personal stamp on it. The best three ways to build your name brand are: 1) Know yourself 2) Choose work that allows you to do your personal best and 3) Market, market, market yourself.

Know your strengths

What are you good at? Why do other people like your work? What areas can you improve upon? If you are not sure what you are good at, how can you expect other people to take you seriously?

Know your niche

What makes you unique? How can you position yourself in your niche market? What value do you provide that makes you stand out? Become focused, do what you do well.

Register your name

Register your trademark or servicemark at www.uspto.gov. Get a business license. Register your website at domain registration at www.networksolutions.com. Having all of your "names" officially registered is very important to protect yourself against copyright infringement, plagiarism, in short; the stealing of your identity.

Gain credibility

What can you do to make yourself an authority in your chosen field? Write a book? Give a speech? Join an association? Putting yourself out there in front of the public is essential.

Develop and maintain your network
Who do you need to stay in contact with? Who can you connect with in the future? What relationships can you nurture that can be mutually beneficial? Word-of-mouth advertising is the most powerful and influential advertising there is.

The second way to build your brand is by the projects that you take on. When you work for yourself, you have the freedom to choose the work you do, so it is very important that you take on projects that reflect the kind of brand you are building. Make your work the difference between ordinary and extraordinary. Do the little "extras" that make you stand out. By choosing work that is important to you and making your projects extraordinary, you make (and leave) your mark. Keep your eyes and ears open. Always be on the lookout for projects, companies, and people that you can bring your special qualities or brand to. Great work does not magically appear. In fact, some projects may, at first, seem dull and boring, but when you perform *your* magic, those projects become exciting. And soon, by word of mouth (and because of your reputation), people will come looking for you.

The third way to build your brand is to actively promote yourself through print and Web-based marketing materials. You can develop professional marketing materials within an economical budget. Make sure your materials are up-to-date, of high quality, contain excellent content, and are readily available to potential clients. It is also important to keep a current read on the marketplace. Is your brand making the impact you want? Do you need to make some adjustments? Do you need to reinvent yourself? Being the CEO of *You, Inc.* is a tough job, but the rewards certainly outweigh the drawbacks.

Develop Marketing Materials
____   Attractive business cards, letterhead, etc.
____   Your own website.
____   A personal biography.
____   Brochures and fliers.
____   Video or audio clip, if relevant.
____   Use testimonials or case studies of those who have benefited from you or your work.

____   Develop interesting story ideas that can be picked
up from the media.

____   Become well known in your career field by writing
or presenting your work to professional associations.

____   Have an effective communication program, so that people
can find out about you (word of mouth, information line, etc).

____   Use similar colors, logos, and messages in your marketing
materials, so people can easily make a connection between
you and your work.

____   Develop a logo and tag line (For example: Get Smart!'s logo
is the knowledge tree with a man and woman reading under it).
And has the tag line: *Educate and Empower Yourself*

Get Smart!
➡ Building a brand is about building recognition, and above all,
trust. Make sure your clients and customers can trust you to do the
job and do it well.

Journal Assignment #12
If you were to own your own business, what would it be? What kind
of branding strategy could you develop to market your business? What
things could you start working on now?

Chapter Nine

Career Killers

"Between saying and doing, there is a long road."
—Spanish proverb

Attitude and Aptitude

W. Clement Stone once said, *"There is really a very little difference between people; it is called attitude; and it makes a really big difference. The big difference is whether it's positive or negative."* To be sure, when it comes to the modern world of work, your attitude can make or break you. In fact, whenever employers are polled about desirable employee characteristics, "attitude" consistently ranks in the top five. To be successful, you need to have the right attitude and the right aptitude. The right attitude means you focus on the positive, are willing to work as part of a team, and strive to be a "can do" person. The right aptitude means having the required set of skills needed to perform a particular job. The difference between the two is that unlike attitude, which is hard to learn, people can be taught basic office skills such as handling telephone calls, inputting customer orders, and how to use a computer program. But it is more difficult for people to be taught to have a better attitude. It has to be a quality that the individual develops on his or her own.

When we think about a "bad attitude," there are many examples that come to mind. One negative attitude that is becoming more common is the feeling of entitlement. Some people think they are automatically entitled to a good job, a fat paycheck, and a fancy lifestyle. But the problem is they don't want to work for it. Another negative attitude is lack of commitment. People will job jump for many years thinking the grass is greener somewhere else. The problem is they take their bad attitude with them wherever they go and invariably end up quitting at the drop of a hat.

A judgmental attitude of self or others is also extremely negative. We fall into the trap of saying, "She's only a secretary." We place judgments on what jobs are considered to be "good/desirable" and those that are "bad/undesirable." But the truth is that *she* enjoys being a secretary, and is even a very good one. In reality, she is exactly where she needs to be at that moment and feels fulfilled by her work.

Our ego may tell us we're too good to do a particular kind of work. If we say this to ourselves long enough, we start to believe this nonsense, and eventually develop a bad attitude about our job. Of course, our work suffers. You can see it everywhere in the workplace. People who are unmotivated to do a good job. People with big bad attitudes who think they are "too good" to serve others with care and respect.

Meaning is not just found in the work itself, but in the approach to the work—the attitude and energy that goes into it. *You* must assign meaning to each of life's moments, no matter what kind of work you do. For example, when I was working my way through college, I enjoyed my job as a waitress, but at the time, I thought it was "beneath" me. This was clearly my ego judging my work. Now I realize that this was the kind of job I needed at that time in my life, and I also learned valuable skills like, teamwork and customer service, that I apply today to my teaching and writing endeavors.

Thankfully, I "got smart" and now realize that Spirit values all kinds of work. And that I can be happy doing anything as long as I am able to share myself and help others. But it is up to me to find the personal meaning in the work that I do. We are starting to realize how detrimental bad attitudes and big egos are to the workplace. The ego gets stuck in narrow titles. Spirit opens to more flexible descriptions. The old way to categorize employees was to rank and separate people from each other, according to their level in the organization. The new way is to bring people together according to their role in the organization. For example, *Fast Company Magazine* has a great feature column where they highlight new titles, like "the Princess of Persuasion," (formerly known as marketing director), and "Director of First Impressions" (formerly known as receptionist). These are new, lighthearted and progressive ways to look at the work we do. When we can call ourselves something interesting and fun, we feel better about our jobs and want to do a better job. (Others may even learn to respect the role that we play.)

The work attitude paradigm is changing. We have evolved from the idea that "work is hard" to the idea that "work sucks" to a more enlightened idea that "work can be fun." But we must first change the way we *think* about work, before we will change the way we *behave* at work. Our conscious choices will have everything to do with how effective we all become on the job, and in our lives. Let's change our attitudes and work together with cooperation, consideration, communication, and commitment.

Charles Swindoll once said this about attitude:

The longer I live, the more I realize the impact of attitude on life. Attitude, to me is more important than facts. It is more important than the past, than education, than money, than circumstances, than failures, than successes, than what other people think or say or do. It more important than appearance, giftedness, or skill. It will make or break a company...a church...a home. The remarkable thing is we have a choice every day regarding the attitude we will embrace for that day. We cannot change the inevitable. The only thing we can do is play on the one string we have, and that is our attitude...I am convinced that life is 10% what happens to me, and 90% how I react to it. And to so it is with you...you are in charge of your attitude.

Social Influences in Career Choices

As has been mentioned before, social and economic influences play a big part in the work that is performed by any one community or nation. As a society, we need a major reality check when it comes to "net worth." In fact, a more equal assessment of the value work that is done and qualifications of the worker is called for and long overdue. We need to alter the societal value that we place on certain jobs—why some are seen as more important than others, and we need to have a zero tolerance for pay discrepancies in our society. How can someone who risks their life to serve and protect as a police officer only make around $30,000 a year? I live in Atlanta, Georgia, a major metropolitan city, where violent crime is an everyday occurrence. This past year, our city's police officers, who are among the lowest paid in the country, had to stage a protest to try and get a meager 3% raise!

While at the same time, athletes, and of course movie stars, demand (and receive) many millions to shoot a basketball through a hoop or star in an all too-violent film. This is clearly a sign of our collective, unconscious ego influence on what we deem important and worthy of high payment. Our world would function just fine without major league sports, but how safe would any of us be if we didn't have people willing to patrol our streets and highways and frequently risk their lives to do so? When we start paying people based on their contribution to society, maybe then our children will learn that the lower-paying jobs, like teaching and social services, are worthy careers.

Our career choices are often dictated by what is deemed "hot." Today, "hot" is typically the world of high-tech, cyberspace and the information superhighway. People enter these fields because of the high demand and high salary, which is all well and good if it is really something that someone wants to do. But most people make career decisions based on the expectations of society or other people. We must do what feel right for us and must realize that our true work must be done for the sake of doing it. Then we will begin to associate work with joy and happiness, rather than drudgery and drain.

Reverend Mary Jo Sparry has the right idea:

I let go of visions society dictates for me in favor of honoring my desires. I follow my inner guide. While there are many wonderful ways to create, to serve and to work, these are not all for me. I know I am at my best when I love what I do. Each day the vision becomes clearer. The passion and clarity of my path is acted upon now and manifested as my good in my life and on the planet. My work, my creations, and the service I give are alive, wonderful and unique. There is a power in my work. I am ever creating that which brings joy to my life and to the lives of others. My gift to the world is also the gift to myself and I rejoice in the blessing.

(Adapted from Creative Thought, August 1999).

How can we change the societal mindset that goes against our inner nature, the one that tells us to go for it, when the outer world says, "You can't do that. What about your bills and responsibilities?"

According to William James, *"It is easier to act your way into a new kind of thinking than to think yourself into a new way of acting."* In other words, "act as if" you are already a successful _____. Take specific action toward your goals and your subconscious mind will follow. Inaction is what leads to frustration and career confusion. When you take action, you increase your circulation, complete more tasks/projects and start creating the career you desire!

Following is a list of ineffective work behaviors for employees/supervisors and career killers:

Negative Work-Related Employee Behaviors
- Lack of time management.
- Apathy or rudeness to internal or external customers.
- Continually late or absent.
- Watching the clock.
- Lacking attention to detail.
- Bad attitude.
- Only care about self.
- Expecting the company to "take care of them."

Negative Work-Related Supervisor Behaviors
- Setting a poor example for others to follow.
- Abusing power or privileges.
- Micro-managing others.
- Lacking communication skills.
- Inability to develop and support employees.
- Not treating people as individuals.
- Forgetting to reward and encourage employees.
- Domineering or harsh.

Career Killers
- Taking a job you are not 100% sure about.
- Producing/selling goods or services you don't believe in.
- Failing to take the necessary time to thoroughly assess and know yourself.
- Limiting your job search to traditional methods.

- Staying in your job because of fear or a false sense of security.
- Believing that you will have one job for the rest of your life.
- Burning bridges with people in your network.
- Not taking a holistic approach to your career.
- Personality clashes with peers or superiors.
- Staying too long in the "burn-out" stage.

Scattered Energy and Self-Sabotage

In order to create your true life's work, you have to become focused. If you have too many things going on, you will dissipate the energy and time you need to invest in your work. If you have a lot of mental or physical clutter in your life, or too many distractions, you will not be able to see clearly what is important to you. Do you zero in and out of clarity only to have your life vision get blurry and unfocused again? To bring into focus means *to make clear, to bring into plain view*. If you are unable or unwilling to see your path, how can you find your way?

Think about a time when you were clear about what you wanted and took action to move you forward. You were empowered because your mind was made up. When you are living by your vision and working with purpose, your sight is like a laser beam—you have your target clearly marked. Focus can also impact your energy level. If you are overly "focused" on family or financial problems, you will be unable to create an opportunity to display your work to the world. Also, if you are messy or disorganized about your life, you will be expending valuable energy just trying to stay neat and organized. There is a lot to be said of an orderly life, as it is a direct reflection of an orderly mind.

You have to see clearly what you want and steer a clear path to get there. A blurred vision or cluttered mind means your energy will be too scattered to bring about the necessary changes. Having too many irons in the fire can take away from your ability to make something really good happen. To avoid dispersing your energy, do not start numerous projects that you are then unable to complete. This is one of the most common ways in which people sabotage themselves.

To sabotage means to *deliberately damage, spoil, or undermine efforts*. Whether it may be going back to college to finish a degree, changing jobs, or moving to another state—saboteurs will make up excuses why it "can't" or "won't work out." Or they may blame their circumstance on others.

To find out if you are guilty of this ask yourself if you are spending your energy on things that you really want? Or if you are letting other things get and stay in the way—lack of finances, a bad relationship, the need to take care of others, etc.? You must get clear on what your real intentions are. Most people have good intentions, but unfortunately, they are usually weak and ill-defined. In fact, it takes a *strong* intention— a conviction—to turn talk into action. If you only talk or think about it, what you want is not very likely to appear.

Highly functioning people know who they are, what they want to do, and have some idea of how to go about it. Conversely, low functioning people haven't figured out who they are, what to do, or how to do it. Typically *fear* is what holds people back from pursuing their dreams. There are several kinds of fear: *failure, success, pain, the unknown.*

Fear of failure is about rejection, of not feeling "good enough." If you have this fear, you may be overly concerned with what others will think about you if you don't succeed. Fear of success if the other side of fear of failure. You may be overly concerned about what people will think, and so play it safe, by not attempting to succeed. Fear of pain is about wanting to avoid feeling uncomfortable, either physically or emotionally. And fear of the unknown is about feeling uncomfortable with change. Since most people have a combination of fears, they can get quite comfortable with mediocrity, and therefore do not aspire to self-actualization activities. After all, the more familiar and easier things are, the greater the comfort zone for most people. So why embark on a more meaningful path? Why take risks? Why rock the boat? Because anything that was ever worth anything was a risk, and most of the time (at the time) it was pretty scary!

Personal growth is a continual process of going beyond your comfort zone. By letting go of your fears, you can find more meaning and fulfillment in your life. Fear is actually a signal that you are on the right track, and when you push past your fear, it can be a transformational experience. Just think about it, if fear is the only thing holding you back *then the only thing holding you back is yourself.* Because you have control over your thoughts, you can empower yourself to overcome your feelings of fear.

Dis-empowered people lack confidence, persistence, boundaries. They often feel powerless over their own lives. They may be focused on the future or stuck in the past and are "all over the map" with their thoughts and energies. They often passively wish things would change and have a fuzzy picture of what they want. They fail to listen to their mind, body and spirit. They feel dis-connected and are unable to see their own influence. Dis-empowered people's beliefs do not match their actions. For example, a dis-empowered person may say that they honor being healthy, but will eat poorly, neglect to exercise, drink or smoke heavily. Obviously, they are not really living what they say is right or important to them.

Empowered people have confidence, persistence, and appropriate boundaries with others. They know they have power over their own lives. They make every effort to live in the present moment, to focus their thoughts and dispense their energy where it needs to be. They use active visualization and affirmation to gain a clear picture of what they want. They are in sync with their mind, body, and spirit and are able to recognize and honor their influence. An empowered person will strive to do the work that allows them to express their authentic self, their creativity, and their love. For instance, a young man attending veterinary school would state his intention this way: "*I live out my dream of working as a veterinarian so that I may help and care for animals and their families.*" And then they will act as if they already are what they want to be.

Journal Assignment #13

Is your work attitude positive or negative? What could you do to improve your attitude? How have you sabotaged your career in the past? In what ways can you empower yourself to create your life's work?

Chapter Ten

Self-Marketing Tools

"Carpenters bend wood. Fletchers bend arrows.
Wise men fashion themselves."
—Buddha

In marketing, it has been said that it takes consumers at least three times seeing or hearing the same message, until they make a connection with the product. Likewise, in the job search process, you are marketing yourself through your resume, cover letter, interview, thank-you letter, and any other career correspondence. Self-marketing tools are like mini-advertisements, in that each time someone gets one of your resumes or meets you in person, it serves to help them remember you. In order to market yourself, like any other product—you have to know what you have to offer—what makes you the "best buy."

One excellent way to begin creating your ideal career is to write and talk about it. The more communication you have with your customers or future employers, the better. Of course, you have to be aware of what you have to offer them. Knowing your skills and accomplishments is a good start.

Skills & Accomplishments

Before you can begin to develop effective Self-Marketing tools, you need to be fully aware of your **knowledge, skills, abilities (ksa's)**. A skill is any identifiable ability that employers value and are willing to pay for. There are three kinds of skills: *personal, industry- specific, and trans-*

ferable. A personal skill is a characteristic that you possess, for instance: being punctual, being honest, or having a high work ethic. An industry specific skill is related to something you learned, for instance, working on an IBM computer, using a spreadsheet software program or knowing how to transfer telephone calls on a 10-line telephone system. A transferable skill is a personal or industry specific skill that you can take with you to a new position, for instance, organizational or time-management. Sometimes skills fall into more than one category, for instance, communication skills is a personal and transferable skill. Knowing your skill set can greatly assist you in doing the kind of work you want to do.

An accomplishment is something that you have achieved, that you look on with pride and satisfaction. And it can be ordinary or extraordinary depending on the person. For example, it may be ordinary for one person to graduate from college, while for another it might be extraordinary because they are the first person in their family to have accomplished it. When it comes to accomplishments, don't sell yourself short. There are many things that you do in any given day or week that are worthy of praise. Think of the patience it took to house-break your puppy or the conflict management skills used on your family members. Employers and customers believe that past successes are a reliable indicator of how well a person will do in the future. Being aware of your personal and professional skills and accomplishments will help you to not only write your marketing materials but to also give a great interview.

Journal Assignment #14
Thinking about your life's work, write out your skill set, categorize your skills according to personal, industry specific, and transferable. Then write a list of personal and professional accomplishments. Consider how each accomplishment relates to a specific transferable skill. Example: "Can keep a balanced checkbook" is translated into *accounting skill.*

How & Why to Write a Resume

A resume is more than just a resume, *it is a direct reflection of you*. When writing yours, keep in mind what you think people need to know in order to form a favorable impression of you. A well-written resume is a like a detailed map of not only where you have been, but also where you want to go. The reader must be able to clearly see why you are headed in a particular career direction.

Resume literally means *"summary."* Contrary to popular belief, resumes are not meant to tell your life story. In fact, it should be an abbreviated history of what you have done that is related to the position you seek. The purpose of the resume is a *sales/marketing tool*— a paper "picture" of you— highlighting your work experience, education, and skills. A resume should stress the positive and downplay the negative. You do not write one to tell your work history, but *to sell your work history.*

A resume is your first and possibly only contact with an employer, so be sure yours is error-free, well organized, and presents you in the best possible light. A resume's goal is to make the person reading it want to personally interview you. Thus, it is a critical initial step in any successful career search, even if you want to be self-employed. Be sure to keep your format consistent in style, paying close attention to the verb phrases.

Keep in mind that you will not write one version of your resume and be done. You must take time and attention with it— write, think, edit, and re-write some more until it is just right. Remember that a resume is a work in progress, you will continually update and change it. You may even want to write a "future resume" to include things that you would like it to say as your career progresses.

Resume Formats

There are a few types of resumes: Chronological, Functional, Combination, and Computer-Ready. The **Chronological** style is most common for people who have held only a few jobs in their lifetime. It emphasizes "when" you worked, and is written in order of the most recent position, going backwards. It describes your duties and accomplishments for each position. This is the most typical format and the easiest to write. Bear in mind, if you have been a "job jumper," choose the three to four most recent, relevant jobs and list them, so long as you can effectively account for any "black holes" of time.

The **Functional** style is used by people with several years of experience in a variety of business or industries. It emphasizes the "what" of what you know, highlighting the skills that you have developed over the years. It places the emphasis on what functions/skills you can perform. The advantage to this style is that it downplays frequent job jumps. It is less common than the chronological style but is gaining in popularity.

The **Combination** style combines elements of both the chronological and functional styles, i.e. the "when and the what" in one format. Career changers often choose this style which emphasizes transferable skills. It is the least common of the styles.

The **Computer-Ready** style is formatted in ascii format, with limited "bells and whistles" (use of **bold**, *italics*, or <u>underline</u>). It be easily sent via e-mail or scanned through an optical character recognition machine. A computer-ready resume is "read" by artificial intelligence and creates a database of the applicant's relevant skills, degrees, and achievements in the form of key words. Employers then access the resume by searching for key words. When writing keywords use nouns instead of verbs. For example, "management" as opposed to "managed."

Computer-Ready Resume Smart Tips
- Keep it simple.
- Use **boldface** or all CAPS for emphasis instead of <u>underlining</u> or *italics.*
- Avoid graphics.
- Do not double space within sections.
- Print it on light-colored paper, one side only.
- To describe your skills and accomplishments use the language of your profession and include key words and phrases.

Sample Key Words for Computer Style Resume
For an accountant: accounts payable and receivable, forecasts, inventory, payroll, controller, B.S. Accounting, CPA, CYMA, Lotus 1-2-3

For a nurse: CAN, Substance abuse, BCLS certification, ICU, nursing home, rehabilitation,
LPN, MSN, I-V experience

A Curriculum Vitae or CV is a longer, more detailed history of your professional career. It is used most often by academics and includes sections on teaching experience, publications, presentations, research projects, and the like. "CV" is also the term used in European countries to refer to a resume. Unlike the resume, career objectives or summaries are rarely used, personal pronouns are acceptable and the length is open-ended. It is also o.k. to have personal information listed on an international CV. Academic CV's usually have listing of professional recommendations.

Smart Tip
➡ Be careful to use correct tense when describing your duties. Use present tense if you are currently performing the duties. Use past tense if you performed them in previous jobs.

Smart Tip
➡ You should also keep a comprehensive, updated copy of all of your jobs held, goals achieved, etc. This document is called a *Historical Resume*, and you can refer to it whenever you need to update your resume.

Get Smart!
➡ Tailor your resume to the position you are applying for.

Must Haves on a Resume
Heading: Provides your contact information: name, address, telephone number/fax number, and e-mail.

Objective or Summary: The **Objective** states what position you are seeking in as few words as possible. It also sets the tone for the resume and gives it a point of reference, which makes it easy to decide what to include and what to leave off of the resume. The phraseology should be short, straight-forward, and specific. The basic formula for writing an objective is to make it concrete and specific, use key words related to your career field, and support your objective with the rest of your resume. *An objective is common for the new professional.*

The **Summary** is a snapshot of what you have to offer an employer. It can range from one line to one paragraph. From the summary, the reader should be able to ascertain what kind of position you are seeking. *A summary is common for the seasoned professional.*

Sample Objectives

Graphic Design position utilizing my creativity, communication, and computer skills

Financial Analyst position involving the monitoring and maintenance of portfolio investments

A sales position within the commercial real estate market

Entry-level customer service position in the telecommunications industry

Middle grade school teaching position utilizing classroom management, presentation, and technical skills

Objectives should also be specific. An example of an increasingly specific objective:

1st level:	Seeking an accounting position
2nd level:	Seeking a junior level accounting position
3rd level:	Seeking a junior level accounting position with a Big 6 firm
4th level:	Seeking a junior level accounting position with a Big 6 firm located in the Southeast
5th level:	Seeking a junior level accounting position utilizing communication and technical skills for a banking institution (located in the Southeast)

Smart Tip
➡ Change your objective line, as needed, to make it specific for each job or job field you are applying for.

Sample Summary

Proven track record Sales Manager with ten years experience working in the high-end residential real estate market. Offering excellent sales, communication, and technical skills.

or

Offering ten years of training and development expertise in the health industry, bringing excellent communication skills, problem-solving, and analytical thinking abilities.

Education: This section includes any college degrees or certifications completed. Be sure to include the complete name of the university, city, state, degree, major, minor, date of graduation, and any additional projects or classes related to your desired position. Do not include high school unless you want to "date" yourself.

Experience: As mentioned before, this section is set up in either a chronological or functional format and describes your relevant work experiences. Work experiences do not have to be limited to full-time, paid positions. In fact, you can draw from the many short-term, part-time or internship positions, as well as volunteer experiences, as long as they are related to your objective. For each position, include your job title, company name, location of job (city and state), dates of employment, and brief description of your duties and/or accomplishments. Note: When listing the dates of employment, if you held a position less than two years, list both month and year. If you held a position for three or more years, just list the years.

References: If you have room, write "Available on Request" at the bottom of the resume. And then provide a list of three to five names on a separate sheet of paper with each person's name, title, business address, and business phone. You may also include a short sentence about how the person is related to you.

Optional Components

Highlights or Qualifications: A paragraph or bulleted list of four to five main points that you want an employer to know about you.

Sample Qualifications

- Over ten years professional work experience in the field of sales and marketing
- Excellent interpersonal communication and organizational skills
- Bi-lingual in English and Spanish
- Willing to travel or relocate
- Listing of Computer Skills: Microsoft Word, Excel, Access, Adobe, etc.

Community/Leadership: List any leadership positions you have held in organizations or participation in community organizations.

Computer or Technical Skills: If you are a particularly technical person or are applying for a technical position, you may want an entire section displaying your technical know-how.

Honors/Awards: If you have received more than one, and it is important for the employer to know about, list them in this section.

Professional Memberships: List your activities and positions held in related professional organizations in this section.

Specialized Training: You may have taken continuing education or attended special courses related to your field of interest, list them in this section.

Presentations/Publications: This is a category common in academia, but if you have given or written presentations or publications in your field, list them in this section.

Certifications/Licenses: List any specialized certifications related to your field in this section.

Smart Tip

➡ Write your resume in descending order of importance, so the reader sees the most important information first.

Smart Tip

➡ Tailor your sub-headings. Instead of "experience," use teaching experience, marketing experience. Instead of "skills," use sales skills, computer skills, etc.

Sample Action Words Used on Resumes and Cover Letters

Accomplished

Adapted

Analyzed

Conducted

Created

Demonstrated

Developed

Established

Expanded

Facilitated

Implemented

Influenced

Instructed

Lectured

Motivated

Operated

Performed

Proposed

Recommended

Revised

Simplified

Streamlined

Supervised

Translated

Prepared

Programmed

Achieved

Administered

Completed

Coordinated

Delegated

Designed

Directed

Evaluated

Expedited

Generated

Improved

Initiated

Launched

Managed

Negotiated

Organized

Planned

Provided

Revamped

Scheduled

Solved

Structured

Trained

Wrote

Sample Positive Descriptor Words
Used on Resumes and Cover Letters

Ability, Adaptable, Analytical, Creative, Competent, Considerate, Conscientious, Consistent, Dependent, Detail-oriented, Determined, Effective, Energetic, Enthusiastic, Flexible, Goal-oriented, Motivated, Persevering, Proficient, Progressive, Organized, Reliable, Responsible, Qualified, Resourceful, Technical, Thorough, Versatile

Sample Transferable Skills Used on
Resumes and Cover Letters

Analyzing, Budgeting, Communicating, Coordinating, Counseling, Delegating, Designing, Editing, Helping, Interviewing, Leading, Listening, Managing, Marketing, Motivating, Networking, Organizing, Planning, Problem-Solving, Public Speaking, Promoting, Recruiting, Selling, Speaking, Training

Resume Do's
- *Include complete contact information*
- *Highlight unique skills: foreign languages, computer hard/software, willing to travel/relocate*
- *Write references on request*
- *Print high quality off white or white paper*
- *Send the most updated, recent and tailored version*

Resume Don'ts:
- *Include personal information such as height, weight, marital status, or number of children*
- *Include a photo of yourself*
- *Bring up salary history (if requested, put it in the cover letter)*
- *Reference political, religious, or personal associations*
- *Send one that is out-dated or sloppy*

Smart Tip
➡ There is no one way to write your resume. There are many styles and variations. Write one that represents you best.

Get Smart!

➡ It is helpful in today's competitive and diversified job market to have multiple versions of your resume, each geared towards a specific position or career field.

Review Your Resume   .

Once you have written and edited your resume, and before you start sending it off, you will want to show it around to several qualified people to see their reaction to it. Just remember that everyone has different thoughts and opinions on what a "good resume" looks like. What one person thinks is relevant, someone else may think is better left off. Ultimately, you are the final judge. As long as you feel confident about how it represents you, that is all that really matters.

Rate yourself or have a friend rate you on a scale of 1(poor) to 5 (excellent).

*Appearance*_____

Criteria: Easy to read, use of appropriate font sizes and styles, creates impact by looking professional, using bullets, bold, etc. Word-processed and printed on resume paper.

Does not look messy, unprofessional.

Does look attractive.

*Content*_____

Criteria: Includes all relevant contact information, objective or summary, education, experience, skills, leadership skills, community service, and professional associations, etc.

Does not seem like a life history, going all the way back to high school and before.

Does contain "need to know" information.

*Focus*_____

Criteria: Demonstrates ability to do the job, supports your stated objective, indicates sufficient knowledge, skills, and abilities required for your intended career field.

Does not include every single position ever held.

Does focus on the position applied for.

*Organization*_____
Criteria: Appropriate format including keywords, phrases/language of industry, is written in logical format (most important information first), not longer than two pages, unless CV.
Does not look "out of order" or questionable in any way.
Does look well-laid out and neat.

*Writing Style*_____
Criteria: Begins sentences with powerful action words. Uses brief, succinct language, free of grammatical, spelling, punctuation, and typographical errors. Content is related to position to which you are applying for.
Does not contain any errors or misspellings.
Does show an ability to communicate.

Smart Tip

➡ A good indicator of how much impact your resume has is to ask others to read it, and if they would be interested in interviewing you.

■ Sample Chronological Resume

MARY HITE
99 Lady Lane, Cincinnati, OH 41000
(606) 555-1111
mhite@internet.com

OBJECTIVE

A Human Resource Specialist position utilizing strong communication, leadership, and organizational skills

EDUCATION

Master of Science   May 2000
Human Resource Management
University of Louisville, Louisville, KY

Bachelor of Arts   June 1996
Business Administration
University of South Carolina, Columbia, SC

EXPERIENCE

Human Resource Generalist

08/96-present

Kentucky Mutual, Louisville, KY

- Recruit, interview, and select 50% of the sales workforce.
- Train and advise senior management in hiring, retention, and promotion of employees.
- Update and write new job descriptions and recommend appropriate pay rates.
- Designed, edited, and produced personnel and benefits manual.
- Developed innovative on-line application and recruitment process.

Accomplishment: Received "New Professional Award" from Human Resource Association.

Human Resource Assistant

05/93-06/96

Southern Bell, Columbia, SC

- Pre-screened all customer service applicants.
- Write and advertised job descriptions for various positions.

- Assisted HR Manager with employee benefit programs.
- Administered typing and customer service tests to applicants.

Accomplishment: Recognized for innovative employee recruitment programs by supervisor.

Front Desk Concierge

09/92-05/93

Radisson Hotel, Columbia, SC

- Assisted customer's with various needs: accommodations, dining, taxis.
- Interacted with other employees in a fast-paced team environment.
- Supervised three other front desk employees.

Accomplishment: Received raise and promotion after six months of employment.

COMPUTER SKILLS

WordPerfect, Microsoft Word, Lotus1-2-3, Windows environment, JobChoice
Electronic Recruiting Software, and Internet

PROFESSIONAL ASSOCIATIONS

Secretary, Cincinnati Human Resource Association
Member, National Association of Human Resource Managers

References Furnished on Request

■ Sample Functional Resume

Sandy Powell

123 Apple Street, Columbus, GA 30001
(706) 555-2001
sandyp@internet.com

Objective

Customer Service position in the health industry utilizing excellent communication and computer skills

Qualifications

- Over five years professional customer service experience in a medical environment
- Knowledge of MS Word, Excel, Access, PowerPoint, and www
- Excellent interpersonal communication and organizational skills
- Bi-lingual in English and Spanish
- Willing to travel or relocate

Areas of Expertise

Customer Service

- Performed all aspects of front-desk operations in a busy doctor's office.
- Interacted with a diverse customer base to ensure customer satisfaction.
- Effectively handled patients' paperwork including insurance claim forms.
- Communicated with customers over the telephone and face to face.

Communications

- Operated switchboard, facsimile, copy and adding machines.
- Conducted meetings with staff members to enhance inter-communication and working relationships.
- Created internal communications system which increased internal communications by 50%.

- Utilized computer to send, receive, store, and retrieve information.

Management
- Supervised an administrative staff of three.
- Interviewed, hired and trained new staff members.
- Ordered necessary inventory including paper products and office equipment.
- Managed accounts receivables and payables.

Work History

Office Manager, Dr. Yio, Columbus, GA	10/99-present
Receptionist, Emergency Outpatient Center, Columbus, GA	06/97-10/99
Customer Service Representative, Target, Aiken, SC	02/95-05/97

Education

Certification, Customer Service Specialist Columbus Technical Institute,	05/00
Columbus, GA *Associate in Arts* Aiken Area Community College, Aiken, SC	12/95

References Available on Request

■ Sample Combination Resume

Sheila L. Stark
Stark@email.com
521 East Bay, Miami, FL 92001
T: (305) 281-4600 F: (305) 281-4601

CAREER SUMMARY

Marketing/business development executive with national experience in customer-direct and web-based marketing. Proven initiator and strategic thinker with effective leadership, analytical, organizational and communication skills. Professional strengths include building client relationships, creating direct marketing campaigns, and developing web-based marketing strategies.

PROFESSIONAL EXPERIENCE

Senior Marketing Manager, Adecca Furnishings Inc., Miami, FL
1997-present
Marketing Skills
* Launched new products, wrote strategic plan, and directed all marketing projects.
* Directed creative process for collateral, media, training tools, point-of-purchase merchandisers and consumer promotions.

Management Skills
* Managed marketing budget of $1 million dollars.
* Supervised and supported field sales team of eight covering four regions across the United States.

Accomplishment: Exceeded sales goals over 10% for four consecutive years.

Product Manager, Office Equipment Direct, Atlanta, GA   1993-1997
Marketing Skills
* Developed print promotions and managed merchandising for 10 retail stores located in the Southeastern United States.
* Created web-based presence and increased sales by 30% in 1st year.

Communication Skills
* Consulted with members of management and technical support to launch a comprehensive, interactive website.
* Recruited and supervised sales force of five.

Accomplishment: Promoted to Manager of Department within six months of employment.

Marketing Intern, Home Showcase, Inc, Atlanta, GA
1992-1993
Creativity Skills
- Created unique ad campaign targeted to college students which resulted in a sales increase of 50% for that population.
- Designed and wrote internship manual for company internship program.

Sales Skills
- Conducted in-person sales demos for organizations interested in office furniture and equipment.

EDUCATIONAL BACKGROUND
Master of Business, May 1993
Georgia State University, Atlanta, GA
Graduated with honors
Specialization: Marketing

Bachelor of Arts, May 1990
University of California, Santa Barbara, CA
Dean's List
Major: Business
Minor: Psychology

PROFESSIONAL ASSOCIATIONS
Member, American Marketing Association
Vice President, Florida Marketer Association

COMPUTER SKILLS
Microsoft Word, Access, Excel, PowerPoint, HTML, Adobe Illustrator

REFERENCES ON REQUEST

Smart Tip
➡ A resume does not have to be limited to one page. If it takes two pages, then by all means give' em two pages.

■ Sample Computer-Ready Resume

KATE KNIGHT
1000 Beach Blvd.
Miami, FL. 940002
(941) 333-0000
knight@email.com

Summary

Over twelve years of progressively responsible experience in sales and customer service. Excellent interpersonal communication and sales skills. Currently seeking a sales management position for a major hotel chain located in the southeastern U.S.

Experience

Westin Hotels, Miami, FL   1994-present
Concierge Manager: Responsible for overall guest services and public relations. Supervise four other employees, which involves hiring and scheduling. Manage guest lounge area, including ordering of supplies and maintenance of inventory.

Marriott Hotels, Atlanta, GA   1991-1994
Banquet Manager: Managed entire food and customer service operations for banquet services department. Supervised three other employees. Ordered and kept track of all supplies. Worked directly with guests to coordinate special events.

MCI Worldcom, Inc.   1989-1991
Sales: Performed direct sales for telecommunications service. Handled customer relations over the telephone and face to face. Consistently exceeded my sales goals. Promoted to Sales Trainer after one year of employment.

Education

Bachelor of Science   1988
University of Georgia, Athens, GA
Major: Business   Minor: Psychology

Associate of Arts   1986
Atlanta Community College, Atlanta, GA
Major: Liberal Arts

References Furnished on Request

Smart Tip
➡ Keep this resume style basic. Avoid using fancy fonts, italics or underlining.

■ Sample Curriculum Vitae

Samantha Tilly

3300 Brookhollow Drive, Austin, Texas 90055

(270) 737-1199

stilly@email.com

Education

PhD. in Human Development, June 2002

University of Texas-Austin, Austin, Texas

Dissertation Topic: *Career Development in Women*

Advisors: Bill Lance, Susan Dillard, Rick Hall

My dissertation is a modern analysis of the changing role
of women in the workplace.

It looks closely at how women are balancing a career and family and generates a new theory of career development. The defense is scheduled for
May 2001.

M.Ed. in Student Development, May 1996

University of South Carolina, Columbia, South Carolina

Emphasis: Career Development and Counseling

Advisor: Julie Nerber

B.S. in Interpersonal Communication, November 1992

Ohio University, Athens, Ohio

Minor: Psychology

Graduated Cum Laude

A.A. in Liberal Arts, December 1989

Schoolcraft College, Livonia, Michigan

Areas of Specialization

Career development theory, feminism, and empowerment issues

Awards

Wallace Fellowship, University of South Carolina, 1994-1996

Outstanding Graduate Student Award,

University of South Carolina, 1995

Noel Johnson Leadership Scholarship, Ohio University, 1991

Teaching Experience

Co-Instructor, Department of Education,

University of Texas-Austin, 1999-present

Contemporary Career Development, three credit course

Co-Instructor, Department of Liberal Arts,

University of South Carolina, 1995-1996

University Success, three-credit course

Related Experience

Academic Advisor, College of Nursing,
University of South Carolina, 1994-1996
Advised 400 undergraduate students in all aspects of lower division nursing curriculum, registration and graduation requirements.
Utilized computerized SAM registration system.
Graduate Assistant, Department of Higher Educational Leadership, University of South Carolina, 1992-1993
Assisted departmental professors and staff in administrative duties.
Represented graduate students on advisory board.

Professional Development

Delegate and presenter for the Texas Career Development Association Professional
 Development Institute, Houston, Texas, September 2000
Attended the National Career Development
Association Conference, Pittsburgh, PA
July 2000 (Earned 20 ceu's)
Attended the International Career Development Conference,
Reno, NV,   November 1998 (Earned 16 ceu's)

Publications

"The Student Affairs Job Search," *Journal of Higher Education, 1999*
"Ethical Student Advisement," *Student Affairs Magazine, 1995*

Presentations

Job Search Strategies for the 21st Century, presented at the Texas Career Development Association's Professional Development Institute, 2000
Interviewing Strategies, University of Texas-Austin Career Center, 1999

Research

Conducted qualitative research on 500 women for dissertation topic based on modern career development issues and concerns.

Recommendations

University of Texas-Austin

Dr. Bill Lance, Department of Human Development   (703) 888-2300
Dr. Susan Dillard, Department of Human Development   (703) 878-3400
Dr. Rick Hall, Department of Human Development   (713) 868-3450

University of South Carolina

Dr. Julie Nerber, Department of Higher Education (803) 777-3100
Dr. Bob Schwartz, Department of Higher Education (803) 777-2100
Dr. Karen Wilson, Dean of Students   (803) 777-4380

Smart Tip
➡ Write a "CV" if you are interested in research or academic positions.

References

A separate reference page should be typed and available throughout your career search process. Appropriate references include past supervisors, teachers, or anyone who is familiar with your work ethic. You can include one or two personal references, such as co-workers or friends, but they should be *in addition* to your professional references. Three to five names is usually sufficient. Be sure to ask each person to serve as your reference before giving his or her name out. Also provide them with a copy of your resume so when called, they will be reminded of your past experiences and the kind of work you want to do.

On the reference page, put their name, title, business address and telephone number. You may also choose to add a line stating how you are associated with this person, although it is not required.

Smart Tip
➡ Always bring a copy of your reference sheet to your interview.

Sample References

References For

Sue JobSeeker

Mr. John Good
Director of Education
Georgia College
Anytown, GA 30000
(404) 555-0000
(Mr. Good is a past supervisor.
I was his administrative assistant at the college).

Dr. Bob Well
Program Chair for Humanities
University of Georgia
Another town, GA 30001
(770) 666-0000
 (Dr. Well was my professor for three classes
during my graduate program).

Ms. Lucy Law
Manager
Entry Personnel Services
Atlanta, GA 30005
(404) 555-1000
(Ms. Law is my current direct supervisor)

How to Write a Bio

The purpose of the bio is to provide an autobiographical sketch of a person. The bio is utilized by people working in professional fields (with higher credentials) and/or by those who give frequent presentations or speeches. However, it is more commonly being used by people who want to present themselves in a different way. A bio is usually three to five paragraphs. The bio highlights the background of the person, including work history, education preparation, and specific projects performed. Sometimes it will include personal information, such as hobbies, interests, or family.

Smart Tip

➡ If you want to stand out from the crowd, include a bio with your application materials.

■ Sample Bio

Steve Sherr

Graphic Designer

As Lead Designer for Creative Industries, Steve Sherr has provided the Marketing and Public Relations Department with creative design services and developed identity programs, newsletters, brochures, and related marketing materials for company image building. He is the webmaster for Creative Industries. His website (www.creativeindustries.com) received an award of excellence in 1999 from the Web Avertising Association of Georgia.

For clients, Steve has created marketing materials for numerous mixed-use, office, resort, and special facility projects including Motorola Corporate Headquarters, Hilton Head Island and Resorts, Coca Cola Enterprises, and for many organizations located in the southeastern United States. He has collaborated with various marketing and design teams to create unique and innovative print and web advertising media for numerous others.

During his ten-year career as a graphic designer, he has also worked as a freelancer and graphic designer at Innovations, Inc. His areas of expertise lie in logo development, idea creation, and graphic image implementation. His excellent interpersonal skills enable him to capture the client's ideas and develop them into compelling and memorable images.

Steve is a graduate of the Art Institute of Atlanta and is a member of the American Institute of Graphic Arts and Graphic Artist's of America.

Services Available:
Creative Consultant
Image Building Campaigns
Logo Development
Website Design

How To Write a Cover Letter/Letter of Interest

The purpose of a cover letter is to introduce you and get your qualifications noticed. The goal of the cover letter is to generate interviews. A well-written cover letter should grab the reader's attention, and entice them to want to read your resume. Some people say that the cover letter is as important of a screening device as the resume is, since it reveals how you think and communicate. The style of the letter should be *personable*, showing your communication style, yet *professional*, displaying your knowledge of the company's needs. The focus should be on what you can do for them, not what they can do for you.

The cover letter should be written in standard business letter format (with the company info listed at the top, and your signature at the end). The cover letter should be limited to one page, with three to four paragraphs. It is printed on the paper your resume was printed on. Of course it should be error-free, easy to read, and tailored to each position you are applying for. A cover letter is required whenever you send or fax or e-mail a resume. There are three main types of letters: "broadcast letters," "targeted letters, and "networking letters."

Use the *broadcast* letter when you want to send resumes to 50 or more employers, all of whom have similar functions or titles. Since you do not have a specific job description, you can broadcast your occupational interest to a large number of employers. In a sense you are asking, *"Do you have a job that meets my qualifications?"*

Use the *targeted* letter when you are sending it to a specific person or in response to a particular position. These letters are tailored-made and provide you with the opportunity the employer show the research you have done on their needs. In a sense you are asking, *"Will you consider me for this particular position?"*

Use the *networking* letter when you are researching the names of people and companies related to your career interest. These letters are usually sent to someone that you know through your network, either directly or indirectly, and can be useful when making a career change. In a sense you are asking, *"Do you know of anyone who could use my skills and talents?"*

There are two other kinds of cover letters: people who are changing careers and people who have been self-employed. These job seekers need to provide very specific information in the cover letter to answer questions that are bound to pop up in the reader's mind. For instance, if your work history is not directly related to the position you are applying for, you need to address this in your cover letter. And if you have worked for yourself for a long time, you will need to sell yourself and build credibility as someone who can "take direction."

Fortunately, your cover letter can be easily changed around, depending on your need. Like a little black dress that can be "dressed up or down" with accessories, once you develop the core (main part) of your cover letter, you can then accessorize it to match the employer's preference. Here are the key elements to an effective cover letter:

1. Contact information: List your information and their contact information.
2. Date and Salutation: Use a colon for formality. Use a comma for informality.
3. Introduction: To spark their interest, pose a question or begin with a great opening line.
4. Body: Provide essential information, your skills, education, experience which match their position requirements. The body can be laid out in paragraph form, or you may want to bullet the main highlights of your letter.
5. Closing: End with sincerity, i.e., "Best Regards," "Sincerely," etc.

Opening Paragraph: Attention
Your first impression comes across with your opening, so include a "hook" to gain their <u>attention</u>. You also need to let them know how you learned about the position.

2nd Paragraph: Interest
You should communicate your <u>interest</u> in the position and refer them to the enclosed resume.

3rd Paragraph: Desire
You should express your <u>desire</u> to work for the company. This is your chance to show off the research you have done on them by making mention of anything that you know about the company and offering a solution to their specific need.

Final Paragraph: Action
This is where you <u>ask for the interview</u>. You want to state something like "I look forward to talking with you personally about my qualifications for this position." Note: Some career experts recommend saying

that you will call in two weeks. If you feel comfortable doing that, go ahead. Just be sure to follow up, as promised. However, I have found that if they are interested, they will call you. Also, be sure to thank them for their consideration.

Smart Tip

➡ Include your telephone number/e-mail on your cover letter. In case your resume and cover letter get separated, they can easily reach you.

Cover Letter Do's

* *Be real, be interesting, be creative.*
* *Send your cover letter every time you send your resume.*
* *Use matching resume paper.*
* *Mail it in a 10x13 envelope to make it stand out from the crowd and avoid creases.*
* *Keep it employer-centered.*

Cover Letter Don'ts

* *Be arrogant, boring, or stuffy.*
* *Use the same letter for every occasion.*
* *Hand-write your cover letter.*
* *Have too short of a cover letter.*
* *Sound self-centered.*

■ Sample Cover Letter-Broadcast

November 10, 2000

Name of Person
Title
Name of Company
Address
City, State, Zip

Dear Exact Name of Person:

With the enclosed resume, I would like to make you aware of my interest in exploring employment opportunities in sales or marketing with your company and to acquaint you with my skills and knowledge.

Excellent analytical and communication skills

As you will see from my resume, I have over five years of professional sales experience gained in the telecommunications industry. In my current role, I provide product information and assistance to a diverse customer base, train others on sales skills, and over-see a staff of ten employees. Recently, I was promoted to Manager of Sales for the DSL/Internet division of Sprint, which is an area that I have a great interest in. Past work experience includes working in the hospitality industry where I learned the importance of going beyond the customer's expectations to ensure their satisfaction. The ability to work well in a team, motivate others, and interest in new technology are only some of the skills that I could offer. In addition to an outstanding work ethic, I hold a Bachelor of Science degree in Marketing from the Ohio State University.

Experience in Public Relations

During college, I financed 100% of my education by working part-time in a variety of positions that involved extensive public relations. Working with the public and my interpersonal communication skills are two of my greatest strengths. When it comes to educating customers about complicated products like wireless telephones, Internet access, and DSL, I have found that it is essential to make sure they understand what they are purchasing and that they know their sales person is a good listener.

At this point in my career, I am ready to make some major life changes. Since I plan to move to southern California area in February of 2001, I am interested in applying for any jobs in sales or marketing that would fit my background. I can provide excellent personal and professional references at the appropriate time. If you are seeking a highly motivated professional with unlimited initiative as well as strong personal qualities of dependability and integrity, I hope you will contact me to suggest a time we might discuss your needs. I can be reached by telephone at (216) 340-0987 or by e-mail at _erick@mail.com_. I look forward to talking with you.

Sincerely,

Eric King

Enc: resume

■ Sample Cover Letter-Targeted

June 1, 2000

123 Apple Street
Columbus, GA 30022
(706) 555-2001

Mrs. Johnson, Director of Human Resources
BlueCross BlueShield of Georgia
3350 Peachtree Rd. NE
Atlanta, GA 30326

Dear Mrs. Johnson:

Are you looking for an educated and enthusiastic customer service representative? Let me take a moment to introduce my qualifications to you. I am a recent graduate of the *Service Industry Academy's* Certified Customer Service Specialist program offering excellent communication, customer service, and computer skills. The director, Mr. Solomon let me know of your need for customer service representatives for your newly expanded call center.

As you can see from the enclosed resume, I offer four years professional work experience acquired in a health-related environment, where I served as a receptionist for a busy doctor's office. In my current position of Office Manager, I assist customers with all aspects of their insurance claims, manage the administrative duties of the office, and supervise two employees. In May of this year, I became *certified* in customer service skills from the Quickstart program offered through the Georgia Department of Technical and Adult Education. During the CCSS program, I updated my computer skills to include knowledge of Microsoft Word, Access, Excel, and PowerPoint.

Through my research, I have learned that you serve a very diverse customer base. My bi-lingual skills in English and Spanish should prove very beneficial in communicating with your Spanish-speaking customers. I feel confident that I am the kind of customer-focused employee that you are looking for and would welcome the opportunity to put my customer service, communication, and computer skills to work for BlueCross BlueShield in your customer service call center.

In August, I will be re-locating to Atlanta and available for your fall training program. I look forward to talking with you personally about my qualifications for the position of Customer Service Representative and can be reached at (706) 555-2001. Thank you for your kind consideration.

Sincerely,

Susie Powell
Enc: resume

■ Sample Cover Letter-Networking

290 S. 3rd Street
Tallahassee, FL 95003
(774) 222-0909
E-mail: riveria@mail.com

September 30, 2000

Ms. Gail Johnson
Public Relations Manager
Disney World
4560 Main Street
Orlando, FL 30505

Re: Public Relations internship position

Dear Ms. Johnson:

From one Florida State Alumni to another, I'd like to take this opportunity to call upon you for assistance/information in relation to the college Disney Public Relations internship, which is offered through the FSU career center.

My experience and qualifications include:
- Bachelor of Business degree, emphasis in Public Relations: May 2001 graduation
- Outstanding overall grade point average of 3.7, while maintaining a part-time job in the university library
- Proficiency with Microsoft Word, Access, Excel, and PowerPoint
- Excellent interpersonal and organizational skills
- Leadership and community service with Delta Omega sorority
- Strong desire to work for an international entertainment organization, like Disney World

If you could you recommend the best route for pursuing this internship, or are willing to pass my resume along, I would very much appreciate it. In addition, I would love to hear how your own career has progressed with the company. I certainly could use any professional advice you could offer.

Thank you in advance for any assistance you can provide. I will call you in two weeks to follow up.

Sincerely,

Beth Riviera
B.S. 2001

Thank-You Letters

The purpose of the thank-you letter is to show appreciation for the interviewer's time, remind them of your sincere interest in the position, mention anything you may have forgotten during the interview, and summarize why you are the best person for the job. Writing a thank-you letter gives you another chance to sell yourself. You may also include an expense statement with your thank you letter, if travel expenses were incurred.

As with most things, timing is everything. You should write your thank-you letter as soon after your interview as possible and send it immediately. It should be brief and to the point, more like a short note. There is more flexibility in writing the thank-you letter than other pieces of career correspondence. You can choose to type it in business format, hand write it on letterhead/stationary, send a thank-you card, or e-mail it. The trick is to do what is most appropriate for your career field. If in doubt, go with the business format. A typed letter should be about half a page long. Of course, you want to tailor your "thank-you" to each person that you interview with.

Smart Tip

➡ *This simple act can make or break you in a competitive race for a prime position.* You may be the one who gets the job just because you took the extra time to simply say "thank you," which translates into consideration and care, qualities employers are desperately seeking.

■ Sample Thank-You Letter

July 10, 2000

Phil A. Fara
6600 Langtree Lane
Atlanta, GA 30000
(770) 777-1000

ABC Communications, Inc.
6060 Rockside Woods Blvd.
Cleveland, OH 20000
Attn: Mark Kane

Dear Mr. Kane,

I would like to take a moment to thank you for the opportunity to interview for the position of Regional Security Manager for ABC Communications on January 28, 2000.

I was very impressed with ABC's corporate philosophy and security management goals. After learning more about the position needed for the southeastern region, I feel very confident that my background in investigations, physical security, and training would be of benefit to ABC's future plans for expansion.

From speaking with you, I learned that the position would require me to "wear many hats" and work in various environments. Along with being very familiar with the Southeast, possessing outstanding teamwork and communication skills, flexibility is one of my strong points. As I have been a small business owner for the past seven years, I have had to perform duties ranging from day-to-day administrative projects to executive long-range planning.

I am very interested in this position and feel strongly that ABC Communications is a company that I could contribute to and grow with. I hope you will give me serious consideration for the position of Regional Security Manager.

Professionally,

Phil A. Fara

Acceptance Letters

An acceptance letter is designed to confirm in writing your acceptance of the position as well as to clarify the offer, starting date, and any unique requirements negotiated as part of the acceptance package (vacation days or professional development opportunities). It is usually written by professionals, particularly those who may be relocating to another city or state. The acceptance letter should be typed in standard business format and sent to the person responsible for hiring you.

Smart Tip
➡ It is wise to put in writing your acceptance of a position, so there is no confusion concerning the acceptance terms.

Resignation Letters

A resignation letter is designed to end your employment with a company or contract. It should be short and sweet. Do not write more than is necessary. There is no reason to explain your reasons in minute detail as to why you are leaving. Remember this letter will go into your employment file, so you don't want anything that can be misconstrued at a later date. This letter is usually addressed to your immediate supervisor and/or to the human resources department and is commonly written in business memo style.

If you had a positive experience, simply thank the employer for the opportunity to work there. If you had a negative experience, think twice before listing your grievances in this letter. If you feel strongly about your negative experience, perhaps a separate letter written (when you are less emotional) may be appropriate.

Smart Tip
➡ It is wise to put in writing your resignation of a position, so there is no confusion concerning your final date of employment.

Get Smart!
➡ There are other kinds of letters you may find useful in the job search, such as follow-up letters, withdrawal letters, and rejection letters. A follow-up letter is sent if you want to remind the employer of your skills and qualifications, and want to further demon-

strate your interest. Withdrawal letters let the employer know that you are withdrawing your candidacy. And rejection letters acknowledge the offer, but respectfully decline. All of these letters are important because every message you send, sends a message about you.

■ Sample Acceptance Letter

March 20, 2000

2001 Barfield Rd.
Tampa, FL 82000
(813) 662-0090

Steve Lee
Senior Vice President
Finance America, Inc.
1000 Peachtree Rd., Atlanta, GA 30003

Dear Mr. Lee:

I am very pleased to accept your offer of an analyst position in the Commercial Finance division of Finance America, Inc. at the annual salary of $58,000. I have had the pleasure of choosing from among several outstanding offers, but it is clear to me that this is the best opportunity in terms of offering a challenging and supportive work environment. As agreed upon, I will begin work on October 1, 2000.

In addition to the information provided regarding relocation, the employee benefits package offered by Finance America, Inc. was a significant part of my final decision. The move to your corporate office in Atlanta was also an appealing factor for me, as I hope to become an integral part of bringing about positive changes in the company.

I am excited to join Finance America, Inc. and work with you and the other talented staff members of the Commercial Finance department. Please let me know if you need any additional information. Thank you for your time and attention throughout the selection process.

Best regards,
Joe Tabe

■ Sample Resignation Letter

To: Sue Garris, Manager
Fr: Mary Cash
Re: Resignation
Date: October 2, 2000

I want to thank you for all you have done for me at Health Mart. It's been quite a pleasure working for you and representing the company as a member of the Sales team.

I have accepted an offer with another firm and have decided to tender my resignation. My last date of employment will be October 16, 2000. This decision has nothing to do with the exceptional opportunity you have provided me here. You and the company have been more than fair with me, and I genuinely appreciate your support.

Thank you for allowing me to be part of your team. I wish Health Mart continued success.

How to Write Classy Career Correspondence

Each piece of your career correspondence represents you, so be sure to leave a positive impression with the reader every time. Unlike face-to-face communication, the reader does not have the benefit of seeing or hearing you. All they have to go on is the way you communicate through your writing. One way to impress them is by providing solid, concrete, real-world examples. When doing this, be sure to quantify your skills and accomplishments by using numbers, percentages and specific dollar amounts to show your results. For example: Trained eight employees on the use of the Smart computer system. Resolved customer relations issues and increased customer satisfaction by 35%. Reduced cost of service calls by creating a new on-line customer service web site which saved the company $40,000.

It is also very important to send your correspondence to targeted employers. Many people waste valuable time and energy mass mailing resumes to hundreds of un-researched companies, only to quickly realize how inefficient this strategy is. Take the extra time to personalize each letter to a specific person.

You can write classy career correspondence by:
- Using correct spelling, grammar, and wording.
- Including relevant information that you want to be asked about in the interview.
- Having a personal, yet professional tone.
- Typing it on a computer and writing it in standard business format, with proper spacing, margins and typeface.
- Sounding upbeat, positive, and professional.
- Tailoring each piece to each individual, position, and company,
- Counting the number of sentences you begin with "I." If it is more than six in one letter, re-arrange your sentences to refocus your emphasis.
- Highlighting what you have to offer them to meet their needs.
- Choosing power words: motivated, results-oriented, energetic, ambitious, creative, etc.
- Developing your own "writing voice," by sharing your personality through your correspondence.

Finesse the Interview

If you are like most people, the mere thought of an interview brings up fear and anxiety. That is because it is often thought of as an "interrogation" instead of an opportunity to exchange important information. The word "interview" comes from the Latin *"inter videre,"* which literally means to *"see about each other."* Because most people get so anxious about the interview process, it is important to keep in mind that interviewing involves a mutual exchange of information based on two-way communication. It is not designed to be a process of inquisition. Generally, the more conversational the exchange of information, the better. To finesse the interview, build common ground between you and the interviewer and match your skills with their employment requirements.

I have found it helpful to practice creative visualization prior to an interview. What I do is take several long, deep breaths, relax my body and mind, and then visualize having a great interview. I see myself projecting a positive image, hear myself providing excellent answers, and feel myself acting confident and composed.

Knowing what the objectives are of the interview from the employer's perspective (as well as your own) is important. For a company, hiring someone is a business decision. For you, it is a life decision. The hiring decision will impact both of you, so finding the right fit is vital to all concerned.

Objectives of the interview from the employer's perspective

To expand upon information contained in your application and resume.

To evaluate whether you would be a suitable candidate for the position.

To provide the opportunity for you and the organization to discuss the possibility of employment.

Objectives of the interview from your perspective

To sell yourself.

To enable you to gain additional information about the organization and position you are considering.

To determine if the company would be a complementary match for your current career aspirations.

Now that you know the interview objectives, let's take a closer look at the stages of the interview process: Preparation, Rapport Building, Presentation, Closing, and Follow Up.

Get Prepared

Keep in mind that the person who gets the job is not always the most qualified or best suited. They get the job because they knew how to finesse the interview. And part of that finesse involves effective preparation.

Anticipate the interview.

Lay out your clothes the night before, get a good night's sleep, take a dry run by the location of the office, etc.

Find out the hiring process for your career field.

How many interviews are required? What is the application process? Are references or tests required? How long does it usually take to get hired?

Research the company by reading up on them in the library, searching the Internet for their company web page, or talking with people you know who work there.

Rehearse your interviewing skills.

You can have a "mock interview" with a friend or a professional career counselor. If you are new to interviewing or not confident about your skills, it is recommended that you video tape yourself. This will give you excellent feedback on your strengths as an interviewee and any areas you need to improve upon. Strive to become as articulate and natural in your presentation as possible so that you communicate readily and easily about yourself.

What to Bring to the Interview
An extra resume, list of references, a professional portfolio or attache case, pen and paper for notes, a daytimer or calendar.

Information to Obtain Before the Interview
- Company mission, values, goals
- Size and potential growth of company
- Product line or services
- Chief competitors
- Organizational structure/culture
- Geographic locations (number of stores, branches, plants, etc.)
- Financial status
- Recent items in the news
- Recent changes in structure or delivery

Where to research the company
Standard and Poor's Register (1-800-221-5277)
Dun and Bradstreet (1-800-526-0651)
Hoover's Handbook (www.hoovers.com)
www.companiesonline.com
Your state business directory
Moody's Manuals and News Reports (1-800-342-5647)
The company's website
People who work or have worked for the company

Smart Tip
➡ Go to your local library and conduct your research there (it's free!).

Build Rapport With the Interviewer

First impressions are vital. The way you present yourself to your interviewer can make or break you! To build rapport is to establish harmony with another person. You can build positive rapport by keeping your composure and remaining confident. The way you present yourself begins with your *appearance*. Be sure to dress professionally. If you are not sure of what is appropriate, ask someone who works there or visit prior to your interview date and then dress one step above what others are wearing. When in doubt, be conservative, wear navy blue, gray, black, or brown.

Women can add a splash of color to outfits by adding touches such as a scarf or necklace. Ladies—don't overdue it! Before leaving the house, count the number of accessories you have on. If you count more than twelve items, including earrings, watch, purse, etc., take something off. Remember when it comes to professional dress, less is more. It goes without saying that you should be neat, clean, and pressed. Both men and women need to go light on cologne and perfume products.

Make Your First Impression Count

When you first meet your interviewer, make good eye contact and offer a firm handshake. Sit down when asked to, smile, and project confidence, competence, & credibility.

Rapport Builders: professional appearance and demeanor, making appropriate small talk, smiling, practicing good body language.

Rapport Breakers: sloppy appearance, poor attitude, being late, no eye contact, slouching, not smiling.

Give a Great Presentation

The bulk of the interview process is the presentation piece, which is your opportunity to sell yourself. This is where you will respond to questions posed by the interviewer(s). There are two basic kinds of questions that they will ask: "What kind of person/worker are you?" and "What skills and abilities do you have that qualify you for this position?" The presentation is your chance to share what your knowledge, skills, and abilities are and is your one opportunity to win them over. On some rare occasions, you may also be asked to role play or present a topic.

Types of Interviews

- **Telephone:** the interview is held over a telephone system.
- **Video Teleconference:** the interview is held via a teleconference system.
- **Test/Application Process:** the interview includes taking a test or filling out an application.
- **One to One:** the interview is one interviewer and one interviewee.
- **Group:** one interviewee with many interviewers OR many interviewees and many interviewers.
- **Demonstration of Skills:** giving a presentation of some kind.

Types of Interview Questions

Standard: are about basic information.

Behavior-Based: looks for your past performance as an indicator of how you will likely behave in the future.

Resume Based: seeks specific information listed on your resume.

Psychological: are posed to see how you will react.

Illegal: are illegal when they are of a personal nature and not relevant to the job.

From *The Blue Chip Graduate,* authors Bill Osher and S.H. Campbell, recommend answering questions like a STAR:

ST...........What was the Situation or Task?

A............What Action did you take?

R.............What were the Results?

■ Sample Interview Questions

Standard
Tell me about yourself.

This should be a two minute oral summary of your resume. The question is designed to get you talking about yourself and reveals what you think is important for them to know. Avoid telling them about your personal life and always end on why you are applying for the position.

What are your strengths and weaknesses?

This should be an easy question to answer. It is designed to find out how self aware you are and what you are doing about any weaknesses you may have. Take this opportunity to highlight your strengths as they relate to the position, and provide examples to support what you say. For example: if you say: "I am very flexible," then provide an example of a time when you had to be flexible on the job. Avoid going on and on about your weakness, simply state one and how you are working on it.

Behavior-Based
Tell me about a time when you took the lead and what were the results?

This question is designed to assess your past performance on the job. You need to select a specific situation where you took the lead and explain the results (remember the "STAR" method of answering a question). The interviewer is basing what information you provide as a means for measuring your possible future performance.

Tell me about a stressful event that took place on the job and what you did to manage it?

This question is a measure of how you typically manage stress and job stressors. They will be looking for specific ways in which you have effectively handled it, such as breathing techniques, taking a five-minute break, positive affirmations—anything that helps you to relax, refresh, refocus (and get back to work). This is an opportunity to show off any problem-solving or creative skills that you possess.

Psychological

How do you describe success?

This question is designed to see how you relate the word "success" to your personal situation. You should be able to clearly articulate what "success" means to you. They are looking to see if you have given it any thought and ultimately what your values are.

Why should I hire you? Or: Why are you the best person for the job?

You should be able to answer this question quickly and succinctly. A good way to respond is by saying: **I am** *(a team player, well organized, etc),* **I know about** *(the importance of customer service, specific computer programs, etc), and* **I can** *(manage difficult customers, perform debit and credit balances, etc). Also include anything specific about the company that you know is a need of theirs, and how you can fill it. For example: "I know XYZ Company has plans for market expansion in Latin America. As you know, I have a bachelors degree in International Relations, speak English and Spanish, and have traveled extensively in that region of the world. I would hope to be of some assistance to you in that effort."*

Resume-Based

Describe your last position. What did you like/dislike about it?

This question is an opportunity to highlight any transferable skills you have that would fit into the present position you are applying for. Be sure to emphasize qualities about your last position that reflect positively on what you would be doing. As always, be specific in your answers. If you say that you really enjoyed the customer contact, be sure to include an example to illustrate it. Avoid talking negatively about the company, your last supervisor, or other touchy subjects. Choose instead to tell them about an aspect of the job that was challenging, and what you did about it.

Why did you leave your last job?

Do not focus on the negatives of your last position. Instead, tell them what you learned from it and that you are now ready to move on because you need more of a challenge, something different, or an opportunity for career growth/advancement.

Illegal
How old are you? Are you a U.S. citizen? Are you married? Do you have a family?

When asked a questions like these, realize you have three options. You can freely answer the question, but may give them an unjustified reason for not hiring you. You can refuse to answer the question, but may give them the idea that you are uncooperative. You can determine their reasoning for asking the question and then respond with an answer that addresses their concern. For example: "Do you have children?" may mean they are concerned whether you will be out of work a lot. In response, you can say, "I am personally prepared to handle the hours and duties of this position."

Other common questions
Describe your most rewarding experience.
What are you long-term career goals?
Tell me about a time you handled a difficult situation?
What do you like about our company?
Describe your ideal supervisor.
What do you do in your spare time?
What is the last book you read?
If you could invite anyone over for dinner who would it be and why?
What do you think is the biggest challenge in our business?

Information to Obtain <u>During</u> the interview:
- Duties of the position/schedule.
- The kind of person who would fit in well with the organization.
- Percentage of time spent on the job.
- Supervisor's name, background, and position in the organization.
- Type and frequency of performance reviews.
- Training and development opportunities.
- Growth areas within the organization.
- Use of technology.

- Career opportunities that exist for someone entering the position.

When they ask, "Do you have any questions for me?" be sure to have a few intelligent questions to ask. It is helpful if you have them memorized or written down.

Sample Questions to Ask the Interviewer

What changes do you see happening with the company?
When and how are performance reviews handled?
What is the history of this position?
What are the success characteristics needed for someone who accepts this position?
What is the management's philosophy?
What is the best and worst thing about working here?
What kind of technology will I be using on the job?
How would you describe the work environment?
What is the company's stated mission and practiced values?
What kind of professional development opportunities exist?
When do you hope to make a decision regarding this position?

Pace Yourself and Listen for Leads

Find out how long the interview may last, so you can take appropriate time for each question. Do not speak too fast or slow. Use an upbeat, interesting tone. Vary your rate and pitch to keep the person engaged. Customize your answers by listening to how the person phrases questions, and emphasizes key words or phrases. Since interviews are tailored to the position requirements, be aware of the key qualifications necessary to do the job and sell your skills to them based on what they are looking for.

Listen to how they phrase questions, as they will often use leads, which will help you to figure out the best way to answer. For example:

Do you think... Requires a logical, analytical answer.
How do you see... Requires an innovative answer.
How do you feel... Requires a compassionate answer.
What's your sense... Requires an action-oriented answer.

Smart Tip
➡ Use key words and phrases listed in the job description, the person's name, and the company's name throughout your presentation.

Keep in Mind Who You Are Talking To

Depending on who you are talking to, different people will look for different things from you.

A *Human Resources* person will screen candidates to match the job specifications.

A *Direct Supervisor* will evaluate your talent, intelligence, and personality.

A *Co-Worker* will seek compatibility and potential contribution to company.

A *Management Team Member* will want to find out if you are someone who can fill a missing link within the company.

What Are They Looking For? (A good match)
- Positive Attitude
- Oral Communication Skills
- Critical Thinking Abilities
- Motivation
- Initiative
- Assertiveness
- Personality Fit
- Leadership Potential
- Enthusiasm
- Awareness of Cultural Diversity
- Punctuality
- Maturity
- Professionalism: appearance and demeanor

Smart Tip

➡ Favorable indicators: They ask you for another interview, talk enthusiastically about the position, give extensive salary/benefit information, or ask when you are available to start.

Who Doesn't Get the Job Offer

Experts say that the most common reasons people don't get job offers fall into these five categories:

Poor Personality (bad attitude, lack of poise and self-confidence).

Lack of Direction (unaware of career interests, no motivation).

Lack of Enthusiasm (lacks drive, monotone presentation).

Lack of Communication skills (inability to express themselves, poor speech).

Poor Appearance (sloppy dress, unprofessional demeanor).

Interview Do's

- *Dress and act the part of a professional.*
- *Offer a firm handshake and make eye contact.*
- *Practice creative visualization and relaxation techniques prior to the interview.*
- *Arrive early and check your appearance in the mirror before entering the room.*
- *Present a positive image, but be yourself.*
- *Build rapport with the interviewer(s).*
- *Ask thoughtful questions.*
- *Put a positive spin on every question, even if you had a negative experience.*
- *Listen carefully and match what they are looking for to your answer.*
- *Show interest by maintaining open non-verbal communication.*
- *Bring an extra copy of your resume and list of references.*
- *Focus on what you can bring to the company.*
- *Be specific and give concrete examples to support your answer.*

Interview Don'ts

- *Arrive looking unprepared or unprofessional.*
- *Carry too many things at once.*
- *Chew gum, slouch, or ask for something to eat or drink.*
- *Give "TMI:" Too Much Information.*

- *Wear too much of anything (excessive makeup, accessories, cologne/perfume).*
- *Go on and on about your personal life.*
- *Talk negatively about your last position or supervisor.*
- *Interrupt or be rude to anyone, including the receptionist.*
- *Do not be the first to bring up salary or benefits during the interview.*
- *Do not focus on what the company can do for you.*
- *Use repetitive speech patterns such as "ummm, uh huh, ya know."*
- *Have irritating habits, such as tapping your fingers, snapping your pen, or twirling your hair.*

Close the Interview

Show genuine interest in the position by summarizing the reasons why you would make the best candidate. "I am very interested in the position of _____ and feel I could bring _____, _____, and _____ to the position. Watch for feedback—what kind of interest do they seem to be showing you? This can give you an idea of where you stand in relation to the competition. Be sure to ask when they hope to make a final decision. End with a firm handshake and aura of confidence. Get their business card so you can write a thank you letter.

Follow-Up

Once you get home, take notes on how you think you did and what things you could improve upon the next time around. Sit down and compose a thoughtful thank-you letter to the person or persons with whom you interviewed. Send it off immediately. If you have not heard from them in the time allotted, it is wise to give a follow up call to see where they are at in the decision-making process.

Self-Marketing Check List

	Yes	No	N/A

- I own a professional suit.
- I am aware of my accomplishments/ skills.
- My resume is updated.
- I feel comfortable writing career correspondence specific to the job I am applying for.
- I have access to a computer, fax machine or e-mail system to conduct my job search activities.
- I have a professional looking portfolio/ brief case to take on the interview.
- I have a separate references page available.
- I have copies of my transcripts, letters of recommendations, and certificates, etc.
- I have a well-developed portfolio.
- I have business cards or brochures.
- I have a website.

Portfolio

Many artistic types, such as graphic or interior designers bring portfolios to their interviews. Nowadays, even job seekers in the business field are putting together portfolios of their work to show. In a typical portfolio, you would display artwork, projects, or papers that you have developed. Even if you don't end up using it regularly in the interview process, it is helpful to create a portfolio of your work for yourself. It can raise your level of awareness of the many things you have accomplished on the job.

Business Cards/Brochures

Many entrepreneurs, freelancers, and small business owners, use business cards/brochures not only for the interview, but also any professional business interaction. Today, anyone can get professionally printed business cards and brochures designed at a reasonable cost. Typically, you would want to put information on it to promote you and your business services. Brochures come in a variety of sizes, shapes, and textures. Remember, that the more colors and the better quality paper used, the higher the cost. Check the Internet for printing companies and costs.

Just Do It!

The key to landing the position of your dreams is twofold: *trial & error and research*. You have to get out there and "do it" to find out what works for you. And, you must learn from your mistakes! You must also talk to those people working in your field of interest and ask them how they did it. Read up on what is happening in your field. Do whatever works in your chosen field. Always project a polished image. Develop high quality marketing materials. When you do get to meet someone with the authority to hire you, you need to have the personal and professional skills necessary to get and hold their attention.

Journal Assignment #15

Update your resume and cover letters so they are the best they can be. What other self-marketing tools do you need to develop for your career field?

Chapter Eleven

The Stages of Career Development

"Nothing contributes so much to tranquilize the mind
as a steady purpose—
a point on which the soul may fix its intellectual eye."
—Mary Shelley

There are six stages of modern career development: *Assessment,*
Investigation, Preparation, Commitment, Retention, and Transition. How
you pass through each stage has much to do with where you are devel-
opmentally in your life. In this chapter, you will learn how your gen-
erational ideas about work, motivation to work, and particular theory
about career development all impact how you choose to create your
life's work.

Generation Gaps

Our world is in a constant state of change and evolution. The state of
the nation directly impacts the kind of work that is performed. Today,
we live in a great deal of uncertainty, ambiguity, and pressure. Modern
workers have different ideas of what work is. In fact, we have only
recently become familiar with the term "career development." I bet if
you asked your grandparents about their "career development," they
would look at you rather strangely. Every individual is socialized into
certain beliefs according to what they learned along the way. Making
sense of your life experiences and your understanding of work requires
becoming aware of your generation's work values and how that may
impact the way you go about seeking and performing work.

Silent Generation: approximately 1922-1943
These folks grew up during the Depression, there was a smaller population, and they valued hard work and honesty.
Boomers: approximately 1944-1959
These folks grew up in the '60s and '70s, and are known for being "anti-establishment," as well as the "Me generation."
X'ers: approximately 1960-1980
These folks grew up in the "Keeping up with the Joneses era," with a serious threat of nuclear war, and the decline of family stability.
Nexters: approximately 1980-2000 (also referred to as Generation Y and Millenials)
These folks grew up in a time of great change and instability, and have an increased use of and reliance on technology.

Each generation develops unique attitudes and values about work, which are formed by their era's societal norms. People who grow up with different economic and political influences will view work from a particular lense. Because of this, our perception of the reality of work differs greatly from generation to generation. Just sit down a Gen X'er with someone from the Silent Generation and you will see disparate ideas about what work is (and should be), how money is made, and what life is all about.

Despite the somewhat negative view that older generations often have about the younger generations in our society, there is much to admire about them. Many X'ers and Y'ers are dealing with crossroads and career transitions, more than any past generation. Because of this, they are more comfortable with change. Characteristics of these groups include being learning-oriented, resourceful, and adaptable. They have a very strong desire to make a difference, a need for choice, and strive for personal whole life fulfillment. They also have a much stronger need for immediate gratification and excitement. Unlike many of the other generations, they are fairly skeptical about concepts such as "security, loyalty, and business ethics."

Another factor in how you develop your career is what work-role you are playing. A role can be defined as *the characteristics and expected social behavior of an individual function or position.* In the modern world, many traditional roles are changing. Take for instance, gender roles—more women are entering the workforce than ever before and taking on the role of "worker" or "provider" as opposed to "home-maker" or "caretaker." Of course, modern men and women often play many roles within a single day!

The roles of student, sage, and master can influence the way you experience work. Work that is performed as a student, sage, or master will feel differently, depending on your level of knowledge and experience with it. People who are successful are willing to change roles as needed. They are observant, and take notice of when to play the student and when to play the master. They open themselves up to more career opportunity because of their flexibility.

Student
This person is just starting out in his career field, is interested in finding people he can learn from, is excited and somewhat idealistic about his field of work.

Sage
This person is well-established in his career field, is interested in moving to the next level or position within his field, and is aware of the positive and negative aspects of his work.

Master
This person is at the end of his career, is interested in teaching/mentoring others in his field, and is beginning to think about future retirement.

People need different things from work at different ages and stages. For instance, a student may need to work just for a paycheck and experience. Or a master may be at the end of his career and merely want to make himself useful. What role are you currently playing— Student, Master, Sage?

In the modern world of work, you will not progress from student to sage to master in a linear fashion, rather you will interweave yourself through each of the roles, depending on your life/career circumstances. Try not to let your ego get in the way of your ability to change roles, because its tendency will be to focus on titles, positions, or status, over the work that you do. For all of us, a critical skill for the new work order is flexibility to handle the many changes coming our way. Sometimes a job is just a job, but it is what you learn from it that matters. If you can take away skills and a positive attitude, you will set yourself up for success for your next position. Each one of your jobs has a lesson to teach, and will move you ahead on your path if you develop positive habits while there. If you are willing to learn from your experiences, become a "student" again, accept a new learning curve, (especially in times of career transition) you will always flourish.

A third impact on your career development is determining what motivates you. Are you motivated to work based on *internal motivators* (morals, ethics, spirituality, self image, sense of accomplishment, desires/passions) or your *external motivators* (money, status, prestige, control, power)? You will enjoy your work more if you are motivated by the internal reasons. You probably will become disillusioned with your work if you are motivated by the external reasons. All too often, people choose careers because of the money or prestige, but soon realize they want or need a different kind of fulfillment, which often turns out to be completely unrelated to material things.

Career Development Theories

There are several types of career development theories. I briefly introduce them here so that you will have a basic understanding of them.

Vocational Personalities and Environments

John Holland postulated that people can function and develop best and find job satisfaction in work environments that are compatible with their personalities. He based his theory on the assumption that people choose careers that reflect their personality. Holland's classification includes personality and work environments: Realistic, Investigative, Artistic, Social, Enterprising, and Conventional (referred to as RIASEC).

Holland also said that the inability to choose a vocation was due to five causes:

1. Insufficient experience to acquire well defined interests, competencies, or personal characteristics.
2. Insufficient experience to learn about the work environment.
3. Ambiguous or conflicting experiences about interests, competencies, or personal characteristics.
4. Ambiguous or conflicting experiences about work environments.
5. Lack of self-information or confidence needed to translate personal characteristics into occupational opportunities.

And that career development problems usually fall into three Categories:
Indecision and confusion
Choice levels: too many and too few
Uncertainty regarding choice.

Developmental Theory
Erik Erikson developed a theory that was based on eight developmental stages that all humans go through which begins at birth and continues until our death. His "Life Cycle" includes:

Trust or mistrust
Autonomy or shame/doubt
Initiative or guilt
Industry or inferiority
Identity or role confusion
Intimacy or isolation
Generativity or stagnation
Integrity or despair

According to Erikson, in order to successfully move from one developmental stage to the next, you must successfully complete each preceding stage. This is important in terms of career development because if you get stuck in a stage, such as feeling guilt or inferiority, it will be difficult for you take initiative or become industrious.

Abraham Maslow developed "Maslow's Hierarchy of Needs" which is a pyramid shaped model. At the bottom lies *survival* needs, then *safety* needs, then *belonging* needs, them *self-esteem* needs, and at the apex, *self-actualization* needs. As we take care of each level, we move up the pyramid towards a higher level of functioning. Unfortunately, in our society there are too many people who cannot get past the first two levels of survival and safety. Creating your life's work often falls into the higher level needs. So, for many people being happy in work seems impossible or unattainable.

People who seek self-actualization have a very strong desire to fulfill higher level needs, such as freedom, growth, independence, challenge, achievement, variety, and meaning. They aspire to fulfill their personal destinies. People who are self-actualized are said to have "peak experiences," they often feel at one with the universe, and have a sense of inner peace.

Donald Super developed the Life-Career Rainbow, in which he theorized about different roles: *daughter/son, student, worker, parent, spouse, citizen, leisurite, senior citizen,* and how each needs to be considered when making a career decision. His basic premise was that people go through changes as they mature, which impacts their career. Vocational self-concept develops through mental growth, observations of work, identification with working adults, and experiences of the world of work.

The average stages of career development according to Donald Super are:

Growth: Birth-15: Forming of self-concept, developing attitudes, interests, and needs, characterized by fantasy, interests, and learning of abilities. Person begins to form an understanding of the world of work.

Exploration: 15-24: Try out through classes, work experiences, hobbies. Collecting relevant information, tentative choice and skill development

Establishment: 25-44: Entry-level skill building and stabilization through work experiences, may advance, and may have to re-learn skills.

Maintenance: 45-64: Continual adjustment process to improve position.

Disengagement:: 65+: Reduced output, prepare for retirement.

Super also believed that we cycle and recycle throughout our lifespan as we adapt to changes in the workplace.

Self-Esteem and Self Efficacy

Our ability to choose or create the career we want has a lot to do with how we feel about ourselves. If a person has perpetually low self-esteem, they will not feel they are worthy of personal or professional fulfillment. Likewise, if we do not feel good about ourselves, we will not feel that we have much control over our environment or life. If we don't feel that anything we do matters or makes a difference, we are not going to be able to do what needs to be done to make it happen.

Albert Bandura defined "self-efficacy" as *the belief that one's actions will have an impact on one's environment.* Self-efficacy can be summed up by how high your level of confidence is so that you can get the things you want from life. If you have a high efficacy, you will believe you can do whatever you set your mind to. If you have a low level of efficacy, you will need to take baby steps—to help you recognize that what you do *does* matter and *does* make a difference. As you build your efficacy, you build your confidence, which will help you to strive for higher goals. Think of athletes. They become confident in their ability because they practice, which builds up their ability, which builds up their confidence. You too, can build your efficacy by practicing what you would like to become good at.

Motivation and Empowerment

Motivation is not only *your desire to do something, but also how willing you are to try, and how long you will persist in trying.* Take notice that most people have a high desire to do things, but do not have the willingness and persistence to follow through and try out several ways of doing it. They are day-dreamers, people who sit around and dream about becoming an actor, a writer, a poet, a doctor, but who never seem to get around to putting their ideas into action. As Yoda said in Star Wars, *"There is no 'try,' only 'do'."*

Empowerment is based on having high self-efficacy and self-confidence, in that you already believe in your ability to carry out a specific task or make a dream come true. People who are empowered are better able to take control of their lives because they believe in themselves, no matter what other people might say. Empowered people have moved beyond survival needs and seek more self-actualizing experiences. They inherently know that they can create the kind of life they want. They have a vision and then take action to create it in the real world. Empowered people are courageous and not afraid to take risks.

People with ambition aspire to reach their dreams and bravely go after what they want. They have high efficacy and therefore are willing to persist through the process. They "will" things to happen, rather than "wishing" them to happen. They recognize *that if there is a will, there is a way.* I believe that *the Will is your Spirit wanting to do something that is right and true and the Way is the higher power that will sup-*

port your efforts.

It is important to know that if you have a great desire to do something, but also have a fear of doing it. you may become immobilized, unable to make changes. The fear will actually cancel out the desire. If you can move *through* fear, you will gain the momentum needed to bring about major career and life changes. Empower yourself by believing in yourself and thinking positively. Remember this sentiment by James Allen, *"You are today where you thoughts have brought you; you will be tomorrow where your thoughts take you."*

Journal Assignment #16

What is one work-related thing that you have wanted to do but are afraid to do because of the consequences? What would be the best and worse scenario if you were to do it?

Chapter Twelve

The Assessment Stage

"He who knows other is wise. He who knows himself is enlightened."
—Lao Tze

Self Assessment

So, you don't know exactly *what* you should be when you grow up? Great! You have the opportunity to discover the many things you could do. As a creative human being, you are multi-talented, and as a social human being, you have the capacity to perform multi-tasks. Why limit yourself by choosing one job or one title when you could share yourself in so many different ways? By becoming self-aware, you can build a solid foundation for your life's work.

Before you move into the next stage (investigation), you have to do some soul-searching. In order make smart career decisions (or any other decision for that matter) you have to know who you are and what you have to offer. The Assessment Stage is where you start the career development process. In this chapter, you will analyze your strengths, weaknesses, talents, interests, skills. You will also begin to understand what is important to you based on your values, and gain information on assessment instruments designed to raise your self-awareness.

In the Assessment Stage, you are getting ready for your life's work. This stage is characterized by unawareness, in that you are not sure what your values, strengths, weaknesses are. You start to feel like you want to know more about yourself and make a conscious effort to get in touch with who you really are.

What Are Your Personal Characteristics?

able to concentrate	fair	punctual
able to manage stress	friendly	rational
accurate	funny	realistic
adventurous	honest	reflective
ambitious	imaginative	reliable
analytical	independent	resourceful
assertive	inventive	responsible
calm	kind	risk-taker
careful	logical	self-confident
competent	mature	sensible
competitive	meticulous	sensitive
confident	modest	stable
conscientious	motivated	supportive
conservative	non-traditional	tactful
consistent	optimistic	tenacious
creative	organized	thorough
curious	outgoing	thoughtful
diplomatic	patient	trusting
discreet	persevering	tough
efficient	practical	understanding
empathetic	precise	versatile
enthusiastic	progressive	witty

Circle your top 8 personality strengths and think of an example when you used them.

Values Clarification

Values are central to our soul. We need to live our lives by them or risk being disappointed by others or out of alignment with ourselves. Since values are so central to who we are, it makes sense to create work that enables us to express ourselves and that allows us to uphold our value system.

Values are intrinsic beliefs and feelings that develop from our experiences, backgrounds, and culture. Values represent the organizing principle of our lives, and are the most powerful motivators of personal action. Some categories of values include: social responsibility, personal development, relationship, lifestyle, work-related, and spiritual/religious.

Much of what we value has been absorbed from others, mainly those closest to us. It is important to get clear on what you value is really what *you* value. Upon reflection, you may wish to re-evaluate your values and put them in different priority. Sometimes, simply changing the priority of your most important values can have a major impact on how you live your life. For example, a person whose top three values are by priority: *Achievement, Balance, and Family,* when they re-arrange the list to: *Family, Balance, and Achievement,* they create a very different life experience, because now they are spending more time and energy on their top value "family" instead of "achievement."

Considering your life's work, make a check by each value that you are seeking:

_____ *Achievement* -the need to set goals and meet them

_____ *Adventure* -work involves risk-taking and excitement

_____ *Aesthetic* -to perform work that is beautiful or
pleasing to others

_____ *Affiliation* -to be recognized as a member of an organization

_____ *Challenge* -to be challenged on a regular basis,
either physically or mentally

_____ *Competition* -to compete with others in a win-lose situation

_____ *Contribution* -to make a meaningful contribution
through my work

_____ *Creativity* -to create new ideas, programs, or structures

_____ *Diversity* -to have diverse experiences, people, and places

_____ *Fun* -to enjoy my work

_____ *Helping* -to be able to help other human beings,
animals, or other living things

_____ *Knowledge* -to gain or impart information

_____ *Independence* -to determine the nature and direction
of my work

_____ *Influence* -to change the attitudes and opinions of others

_____ *Recognition* -to be well-known in my field of work

_____ *Routine* -to perform basically the same kinds of tasks

_____ *Physically Challenging* -to perform work that makes physical demands of me

_____ *Power* -to have control or dominance over
the activities of others

_____ *Prestige* -to have a high status position

_____ *Profit* -to make a significant amount of money

_____ *Public Contact* -to have extensive contact with
many types of people

_____ *Security* -to have a stable, secure work environment
and/or position

_____ *Travel* -to have the opportunity for travel while working

_____ *Variety* -to do many different kinds of tasks on a
daily/weekly basis

_____ *Unconventional* -to do work that is out of the mainstream

_____ *Work Alone* -to work on projects independently

_____ *Work With Others* -to have close working relationship
with a group

_____ *Wisdom* -to learn, understand, and grow in my work

List others not mentioned

_____

Sometimes we are doing things in life because we think they are important. But in reality, we have not even stopped to consider what is really important to us, and find ourselves spending time doing things that are not as important as we thought. The good news is that by reading and working through this LearningBook, you can begin to create your life's work by living and *working* in alignment with your values.

Journal Assignment #17
What are your top three work-related values? Do they match your current work situation? If not, how can you integrate them into your life's work?

Defining Moments and Dreams

To learn about your true desires, you have to pay attention to your dreams and the defining moments that occur in your life. Life events that have happened, good and bad, have an impact on you, and they often take you in a different or unexpected career direction. These events may not only have changed your career path, but may have caused you to stop and consider if your life was the way you really wanted it to be. Defining life moments could also be experiences where you have said, "yes, this is definitely for me" or "no, this is definitely not for me."

A defining moment usually asks you to take a risk, to choose a non-traditional path or to radically change your life direction. People who have experienced such moments know that by choosing the non-traditional or unexpected life, that there is a much greater chance for a more fulfilling (albeit challenging) experience. When you make the tough decisions in life, you must have strong intentions because your unconscious and conscious thoughts are what will manifest in your life. You have to be consciously aware of what you want in order for it to happen. Consider what your defining moments have been in your life.

Case Illustration
Linda was on the fast-track with her career in advertising. She had relocated to Atlanta, Georgia from a small town in South Carolina and had been working for a major advertising agency for seven years, when something unexpected happened. Her younger brother was killed in a car accident. This unexpected life event made her stop and think about whether she was living the kind of life that she wanted. After some soul-searching, she realized that she really wasn't that happy with her work or her personal life. In fact, she realized that she had just grown accustomed to it. Deep down she felt unfulfilled.

With the help of a career counselor, she took a values inventory. She saw that the life she was living, was not necessarily the life she wanted to lead. In fact, for the past ten years, she had been living and working on "auto-pilot." Once she got clear on the life vision she had, she was ready to make some major changes. The first decision she made was to move closer to her family. She then made a complete U-turn in her career direction and decided to become an airplane pilot. Flying was something that she had always wanted to do, but never pursued because of lack of time. Not long after getting her pilot's license, and because she was so thrilled and excited with her new-found passion, she began to teach others to fly. She now soars to great heights every day and helps others to do the same.

Walt Disney, the great visionary, animator, and entertainer once said, *"All our dreams can come true, if we have the courage to pursue them."* This is so true, but we must be bold in what we want and be brave enough to go after it. What are your dreams? You need to pay attention to them, as the unconscious will provide excellent guidance and direction. Your dreams will not go away. In fact, they will keep preying on you until you wake up and get to work! You will think about them all the time, and rationalize that "it's too crazy" or " it would never work." You might wonder how you could actually make them a reality, and even be afraid what would happen if you did. Don't be afraid to follow your dreams because this is your inner self giving you direction. In fact, because dreams come from our unconscious minds, which is where many of our true motivations and intentions lie—they are often the best information we receive. Why not keep a dream journal to capture some of those messages?

When it comes to deciding on a career, consider what you would do if you were brave enough? What can you do to put yourself on the right path? Do you need more information? Can you commit to making a change in order to fulfill your purpose? Or do you just need to summon up your courage? Keep in mind:

1. You must become whole-life focused, i.e., realize that your career is just one part of your life.
2. You must know your values and live by them.
3. You must become aware of your gifts—what you can share with the world.
4. You must choose a vocation that fits your lifestyle.

Journal Assignment #18

Answer the following key questions to uncover your life's work.
In what ways can I express my soul through my gifts, talents, knowledge?
What are my avocations? (Many times you can turn a hobby into a career).
What are my dreams?

"Who Am I?"
My strengths are
My weaknesses are

I have been complimented on
My purpose is to

"What is Stopping Me?"
What barriers do I have to creating my life's work?
What are some past obstacles that I have overcome?
I am afraid or concerned about
I may have to give up_____in order to create my life's
work

"What Am I Good At?"
My areas of expertise lie in
Time flies when I am
Something I am proud of is
People sometimes come to me for advice about

"What Kind of Work Environment Do I Need?"
I work especially well in a _____work environment
I like working with _____types of people
I definitely do not want_____from my work environ-
ment
In work, I have gotten into trouble for

Career Assessments/Tests

If you are still having trouble figuring out the nebulous question of *"Who Am I and What Was I Sent Here to Do?"* you can utilize career assessments. They are designed to help you see clearly what your interests, values, abilities are and your overall personality. Career assessments can give you some direction. I have used several and will share the two that I find most useful. I would recommend talking with a professional counselor to discuss your results, particularly if you took the test on the Internet. A qualified career counselor/coach can give you valuable feedback about your results that will make the assessment much more useful and meaningful to you.

John Holland developed the *Self-Directed Search* (SDS) vocational test which divides people and work environments into six areas.

Realistic, Investigative, Artistic, Social, Enterprising, Conventional
Realistic people like to work with things.
Sample career: Carpenter
Investigative people like to work with information.
Sample career: Chemist
Artistic people like to create things.
Sample career: Musician
Social people like to help people.
Sample career: Counselor
Enterprising people like to lead others.
Sample career: Entrepreneur
Conventional people like to organize data.
Sample career: Secretary

A simple version of this test was developed by well-known author of *What Color is Your Parachute,* Richard Bolles. Imagine you are at a party, which group would you be drawn to talk with first? And second? And third? The three letter code that you choose is your Holland Code. Once you have a code: ISA, CAI, SEC, etc, you can look up matching possible job titles in the SDS manual. For example, someone like me, with a SEA code (social, enterprising, artistic), might be interested in teaching, writing, or consulting types of careers, where they would be able to put to work the aspects of helping people, leading others, and creating things.

Another common assessment used in career guidance is the *Myers Brigg Type Indicator* (MBTI). The MBTI is a psychological instrument designed to describe human behavior. It has been used in many settings from college campus to corporate office, and is a very reliable personality test. After answering some questions, you get a four letter "type" which describes how you prefer to gather data, make decisions, structure your life, and relate to others in the world.

The letters that create an MBTI type are:

E-Extroversion   I-Introversion
(How you gain energy, based on being with others or spending time alone)
N-Intuitive   S-Sensing
(How you perceive the world, based on your sixth sense or five senses)
T-Thinking   F-Feeling
(How you make decisions, based on objectivity or subjectivity)
J-Judging   P-Perceiving
(How you choose to live your life, based on planning it or keeping your options open)

It is helpful to know about the powers and pitfalls of your personality type, as you may unknowingly be making mistakes in your job search. For example, one of the areas that the MBTI measures is your preference for extroversion (E) or introversion (I). "E" types are outgoing and direct, a helpful trait when networking for work. But they could be all talk and no action! "I's" tend to make more use of technology, and may not make as much personal connection in their search. Obviously, you need both to be successful. Another trait is planning or "going with the flow," with the letters "J" standing for the planner and "P" going with the flow. Generally, a "J" is often more comfortable once a decision has been made, but may sometimes jump the gun on the first offer that comes along, instead of waiting for a better one. A "P" is more comfortable when they have options, so may wait too long to make a decision.

Put simply, there may be career fields better suited to you, simply because of your temperament or preference. Likewise, there may be career areas you are interested in, but are not having much success in. Becoming aware of why this may be occurring is extremely helpful, because you can then make necessary changes. For example, some personality types are well-suited for owning their own business, while others are not. (It doesn't mean that those others can't succeed, it just means they may have to work harder or do things differently).

There are various other types of instruments, such as the *Enneagram, COPS/CAPS & COPES,* and the *Birkman* test. But the SDS and MBTI are two of the better known career-related assessments. You can also visit a college career center or career counseling center and utilize other computer-guided assessment instruments, such as the

Discover and *Focus* programs.

Assessment instruments are designed to help you gain greater self-awareness and to provide possible career options. Listen to *yourself* first! Don't become reliant on these tools to tell you what you are meant to be. Tests can *illuminate* areas that you may want to take a closer look at, *highlight* areas you never considered, and even provide you with some possible *career ideas*, but they *cannot tell you what to do*. Just because a test reveals that you have an aptitude to be a business executive, doesn't mean that you want to become one. Instead of focusing on a job title, pay attention to the skills and abilities related to specific jobs to see what patterns you see in your scores. They may reveal where your talents and abilities lie. Then you can figure out how to apply them, according to what feels right for you.

Why do people go to tarot card readers or psychics? To affirm their own inner knowledge. The power of suggestion is incredible. Career assessments can be a lot like a doctor's prognosis. We hear what we want to hear when given our test results. And when we make up our mind one way or the other—to get better or not—we develop a self-fulfilling prophecy. Try not to live out a self-fulfilling prophecy either way, if a test doesn't affirm what your heart's desire is, remember that it is only *one test, one prognosis*.

Just like it is wise to get a second doctor's opinion, it is wise to get results from another test or source. You would never want to base a career decision on one test alone. For example, if a test tells you to be flower arranger, but you really want to become a teacher, then do what feels right for you. Get smart and treat your test scores as pieces of a big puzzle, put them in their appropriate perspective, and add them to your growing base of information, which becomes more self-revealing. Pay attention to patterns or themes that overlap in several different tests. The information gained can be valuable when you get to the point in the process where you begin to make a decision. Always enlist the expertise of a career counselor/coach to help you sort it all out.

Get Smart!
➡ Career tests re-affirm what you already intuitively know to be true about yourself.

Journal Assignment #19

Write out your life story. Include your childhood, challenges, tri-
umphs, and anything you think is important to include. After writing
it out, tell your story to several people, get their feedback, and notice
any patterns that emerge as you re-tell it. (Sometimes the things we are
meant to do come from lessons we have learned in our own life).

Chapter Thirteen

The Investigation Stage

"Opportunities are usually disguised as hard work,
so most don't recognize them."
—Unknown

The world of work is in a state of reinvention. To be successful, you must learn what the modern world of work is like and how it has evolved over the years. You must also research possible careers and find out as much as possible about your career interests before making a decision. The Investigation Stage is the second stage in the career development process. In this chapter, you will learn about career trends, job categories, and how your own position on your career path will determine the next move you make.

In the Investigation Stage, you are still getting ready for work. This stage is characterized by feelings of confusion, in that you are not sure what career options exist for you. You may feel overwhelmed with all of the different jobs and opportunities that exist as you begin the process of researching the modern world of work.

Differences Between the Industrial Age and the Information Age

In the *Industrial Age*, most of the jobs came from industrial and manufacturing fields based on a national level. The job market consisted of "blue collar" workers and "white collar" workers. The way to get a job was to answer local want ads and apply to placement services. People strived to move up the corporate ladder and stayed with one company for life. They worked toward retirement, and looked forward to the day that they would no longer have to work and could live off of their pension or savings.

In the *Information Age*, most of the jobs come from knowledge/service firms based on a global level. Now, the job market consists of technical, service, professional, and executive positions. The way to get a job involves the combination of technical skills and interpersonal networking. Today, people strive to develop more than one area of expertise. People work for various organizations, and even enjoy short-term, contract work. They seek a balance between their work and play. Many want to spend more time living and less time working.

The new worker expects a new world of work. Modern workers are often called "Knowledge workers" because they value learning and independent thinking. They are paid to use put their knowledge to work. The new worker also values authenticity and the freedom to express themselves. They focus more on the roles they play, rather than the titles that they hold. In general, they are actively seeking much more meaning and fulfillment from the work they perform.

Research the World of Work

There are many ways you can conduct your research on the modern world of work. One of the best resources is the *The Occupational Handbook* put out by the Bureau of Labor Statistics. It is designed to make projections on the work opportunities available in the future. For example:

- *By 2005, the number of self-employed workers is expected to increase by 950,000 to 11.6 million.*
- *Service and retail industries will account for 16.2 million out of a projected growth of 16.8 wage and salary jobs.*
- *The fastest growing occupations are in computer technology and health services.*
- *Jobs that require the least amount of training and education and offer the least amount of money will continue to provide the most openings (4 out of every 10 jobs).*
- *The labor force will continue to become more diverse, with more women and minorities making up the workforce.*

You also need to conduct research on the latest career trends. The

Bureau of Labor Statistics predicts that by 2005, due to the aging population, many of the fastest growing occupations fall into the health field. Sample occupations include: home health aides, physical therapists, medical records technicians, occupational therapists, speech-language pathologists, respiratory therapists, psychologists. Other rapidly growing areas are in the information technology sector: computer scientists, programmers, systems analysts, etc.

Knowing how jobs are organized is also helpful. ACT's *Discover* Computerized Guidance Program arranges job families into a "world of work map." The jobs are grouped based on the job's primary tasks, i.e., working with data, ideas, people, or things. There are six general areas in the work world: *Business Contact, Business Operations, Technical, Science, Arts, and Social Service.* Job categories include:

Marketing & Sales
Management & Planning
Records & Communications
Financial Transactions
Storage & Dispatching
Business Machine/Computer Operation
Vehicle Operation & Repair
Construction & Maintenance
Agriculture & Natural Resources
Crafts & Related Services
Home Business Equipment Repair
Industrial Equipment Operation & Repair
Engineering & Related Technologies
Medicine Specialties & Technologies
Natural Sciences & Mathematics
Social Sciences
Creative/Performing Arts
Applied Arts (Visual and Spoken)
General Health Care
Social & Government Services
Education & Related Services
Personal Customer Service

The really interesting thing about the investigation stage is that you have the opportunity to see the many career options that exist. Once you start the investigation process, you will quickly realize that there are endless possibilities. This can be overwhelming at first, but it will be easier than you think because you have spent the necessary time assessing yourself. Now all you have to do is find a complementary match.

Case Illustration
Doug is a 28-year-old bartender struggling to figure out what his career options are. His problem is that he is interested in too many things and has trouble making a decision, so he just keeps putting it off. Since graduating from college with a journalism degree, he has spent the last four years wandering from job to job. During school, he had an internship in public relations and created a website, which he really enjoyed. He also tried his hand at journalism as a writer for the school paper, which he didn't end up liking. After college, he worked in fundraising, the restaurant business, and picked up freelance work as a web designer.

Doug feels like he is "off-track" and heading nowhere fast. So he decided to start getting serious about making some kind of career decision. He has always been interested in owning his own business and he is aware of what his strengths are: creativity, independence, flexibility, and computer knowledge. He is also very aware of his tendency to get bored easily, and his general dislike for a 9-5 job. Based on what he knows about himself, he began investigating possible business ideas that he might like. After researching and talking with several friends who owned small businesses, he came up with two ideas that seemed well-suited: a website design business for small business owners, and an online advice/consultation service for web-related products and services.

Investigate Your Career Options

For a very simple way to investigate your career options, follow this five step process.

1st Step:
Become Self-Aware: Get to know who you really are and review what is important to you.

2nd Step:
Prioritize Your Needs: List the top ten things you need from a career.

3rd Step:
Brainstorm Career Ideas: Make a list within each category or field of consideration (this can be long in length and crazy in content).

4th Step:
Focus on the Top Three Choices: After review, which one(s) seem most do-able given your life situation?

5th Step:
Investigate Your Career Options.

After you have given some thought to what your options are, it is time to investigate the reality of the situation. The best way to do that is to conduct informational interviews with people doing the kind of work that you want to do. In other words, pick their brain.

Conduct Information Interviews

An information interview is an excellent way to gain knowledge about a company or career field that you may have an interest in. These interviews have two benefits. 1) you gain insight into the career, and 2) you are able to meet with potential employers in a pleasant, low-stress environment. Before calling, it is wise to prepare a telephone script. For example:

Ms. Thompson, my name is _____. I was referred to you by_____. I am very interested in the field of training and development, but don't have enough current information to make a career decision. I thought if I could talk to someone knowledgeable, like yourself, I would get a clearer picture of the profession. I would very much like the opportunity to come to your office to discuss your professional views on the trends in training and development, particularly distance learning and technology. Would the first week of September work in your schedule?

If she is unable to meet in person, try to schedule a telephone interview. However, it is preferable to go on site because you can get a feel for the work environment and gain valuable information about the company culture, etc. You should use this time to get them talking about themselves, where they will likely share any bits of wisdom they have learned along the way.

It is appropriate to ask about the interviewing process or employment opportunities they have knowledge of, but remember this is not an employment interview, you are not there to sell yourself—you are there to gain information. If they offer to let you "shadow" someone for a day, take them up on it.

Once you set the interview, come with specific questions, and keep to your scheduled time. Bring a resume in case they ask you for it at the end of the interview.

Sample Information Interview Questions

1. *How did you get where you are today? What has your career path been like?*
2. *How long have you been in _____ career field?*
3. *What recommendations do you have for someone who is interested in _____?*
4. *What do you like/dislike about your job?*
5. *What kind of person would do well in this career field?*
6. *What changes do you see happening in the industry?*
7. *What kind of education and experience is needed?*
8. *What is a typical day like?*
9. *What does the hiring process involve?*
10. *Describe the working environment? Is it formal? Casual? Standard hours or overtime?*
11. *Tell me about a time when you received an award or special recognition.*
12. *Do you know of any upcoming employment opportunities with the company?*
13. *Why do you like working here?*
14. *What is the most important thing for a new employee to know about?*
15. *Is there anyone you would recommend that I also speak with?*

Smart Tip

➡ Be sure to ask for their business card so you can write them a thank-you note.

Get Smart!
➡ Remember you are shopping for a "career fit." You want to find out *all* there is to know about the industry so you can make a smart decision, one that fits you "just right."

Characteristics of Work Environments

Knowing the kind of work environment you would most enjoy can really help you make smarter career decisions. Consider the following options and ask yourself which sounds like the better fit?

Large Company
Traditional option, usually located in a bigger city
Low risk, high pay (salaried positions)
Good benefits, vacation time
40+ hours a week (usually more)
Very structured, with titles, departments, roles, and duties clearly defined
High amount of supervision
A positive is that you can develop social relationships with co-workers.
A negative is office politics.

Choose this work option if you like the "security" of a big company, need to know exactly what is expected of you, and can handle authority.

Small – Medium Company
Newer option, can be located in any sized city
Low risk, varied pay (salaried positions)
Good benefits, vacation time
40+ hours a week (more flexibility in time)
Moderately structured, with titles, departments, roles, and duties defined, but open to change
High amount of supervision
A positive is that there is room for growth, and can perform a variety of tasks.
A negative is office politics.

Choose this work option if you like working for a company, (but want something a little smaller), want to make a contribution, and can handle performing many roles.

Start-up Company
Emerging option, can be located in any sized city
High risk, medium– high pay, depending on the type of venture (salaried plus stock options positions)
Fair to good benefits, may or may not have vacation time
40+ hours a week (overtime expected)
Low structure, with titles, departments, roles, and duties changing daily
Low supervision
A positive is that you work in a dynamic environment and can be a key person in the company.
A negative is that it can stressful and fast-paced.

Choose this work option if you like a challenge, are interested in a dot.com or technology venture, and can handle a lot of change and uncertainty.

Independent Contractor
Non-traditional option, can be anywhere
Medium risk, high pay (hourly positions)
0 company-paid benefits or vacation time
As many hours as you want to work a week (you set your schedule)
Medium structure (your client tells you what needs to be done and then you do it)
High-low supervision (depending on client style)
A positive is that you can direct your own time and choose your own projects.
A negative is that you have to spend money and time developing new business/clients.

Choose this work option if you like a variety of different companies and people to work with, are a good self-marketer, and can handle periods of little or no work.

Entrepreneur
Re-emerging option, can be anywhere
High risk, undetermined pay (very low in the beginning stages)
0 benefits (unless you pay for them), you take your vacation when you want
As many hours as you want to work (may sometimes feel like there is no difference between personal and professional time)
Low structure (you decide when, what, where, and what gets done)
Low supervision (you supervise yourself and/or other employees)
A positive is that it provides a sense of personal accomplishment and pride. A negative is that you are in charge for all aspects of the business.

Choose this work option if you like taking risks, have a good idea/business sense, and can handle being fully responsible.

Where Are You on Your Career Path?
Now that you have an idea of where you are headed, you need to find out where you are on your career path. Once you find this out, you will be better able to navigate your way to your desired destination.

Right on Track: You are progressing as expected and are happy with where you are at now and where you are headed.

Fast Track: You are moving fast along your path and don't have much time to consider if this is really what you want to be doing.

Slow Track: You are moving slowly along your path and are either happy or not happy with your current rate of speed.

Beginners Track: You are just beginning in your career field and are learning the ways of the road.

Totally lost Track: You are completely lost and are not sure which road to take next.

Exiting-off Track: You are at the end of your career and ready to get off the ramp, but still wanting to drive on a part-time or contractual basis.

Where you are at in your career will obviously have an impact on how you make decisions, because at different stages of your life, you will seek different things from your work. Questions to consider:

Are you even driving the right kind of vehicle?

Are you following the "family van?"

Are you getting run over by other "drivers?"

Who is in the driver's seat?

Are you comfortable with how your journey is progressing?

Do you have a map with you or are you winging it?

Do you get easily side-tracked or lost?

Is fear getting in your way of trying a different route?

Is it time for a career tune-up?

Journal Assignment #20

What career field interests you? Who can you talk to learn more about it? Where are you on your career path? What other things will you do to investigate and research your career options?

Chapter Fourteen

The Preparation Stage

"The people who get on in this world are the people who get up and look for the circumstances they want, and if they can't find them, make them."
—George Bernard Shaw

So now you know all about yourself and the kind of work you want to do. The next step is to become prepared for your life's work. The Preparation Stage is the third step in the career development process. In this chapter, you will learn the importance of creating a successful mindset, developing multicultural skills, setting goals, and how to go about gaining practical experience in your field of interest.

In the Preparation Stage, you are still getting ready to do your life's work. This stage is characterized by feelings of excitement, as you think of how wonderful it will be to perform meaningful work. However, there is still much work to be done, and in order to be successful, you have to be prepared.

Attract Success

The "Law of Attraction" means that the universe attracts similar vibrations and frequencies to us through our mental and emotional tones, which are based on love or fear. When we send out positive vibrations, we magnetize only good things back to us. When we let fear, doubt, or guilt cloud our mental frame of mind—we are sending out a lower frequency, and attracting likewise.

Having passion for your work and your life infuses creativity into what you do. If you are doing something that is bringing you joy or passion, you are vibrating at a high rate and are open to the positive gifts. It has been said that *Success is a state of mind combined with a state of readiness.* This observation is especially true for career development. You must have both a positive mental attitude combined with a solid set of beliefs about your ability to set and meet your goals.

Despite what many people think, success is much more about hard work, knowledge, resourcefulness, and perseverance than anything else. People who experience success in their careers know what they want and they go after it with passion, conviction, and hard work. In fact, someone once said, *The only place you find success before work is in the dictionary.* In other words, if you want to be successful, you are going to have to work for it.

What is success and how do you achieve it? Success can be defined as *the progressive realization of a predetermined, worthwhile goal or dream.* This definition of success underlies the importance of having goals. You can't achieve success without developing goals. Goals give life meaning. As humans, we are designed for achievement and accomplishment. H.L. Hunt, who was at one time the richest man in the world, said that he had discovered three steps that would lead to success. *1). Decide what you really want out of life. 2). Develop a plan of action for achieving it. 3). Act, with great enthusiasm.*

Of course, the definition of success varies from person to person, according to what goals they set for themselves. For some, having a career in a particular field, making a certain amount of money defines success. For others, having a career that enables them to make a real difference in people's lives is what makes them feel successful. For others, it is finding their unique life balance in all areas of their life.

I think it is safe to say that most folks who are successful in meeting career aspirations have similar traits: *They are passionate about their craft. They love what they do. They do not give up easily. They are willing to be a lifelong learner. They are open to adventure and not afraid to take risks. They are resourceful—they can find needed information.* As Disraeli once said, "*As a general rule, the most successful people in life are those who have the best information.*" Access to information is what the Information Age is all about, and those who know where to go to log on, download, or tap into technology and information will be better armed for success in their careers.

To attract more professional success in your life, think about it and visualize it. As I have mentioned many times before, thoughts are powerful. Depending on their nature, they can either bring positive things into your life or negative things. What you say to yourself has a lot to do with how successful you are. If you have been not experiencing much success, perhaps changing your mental programming can help. Upload a new software, with new ideas and thoughts! Start by using the "language" of success. Say to yourself and others, "I can do it." "I have marketable skills." "I am a successful_____." What other affirmations will you say to yourself when you start to doubt things?

The process of visualization is a powerful technique to achieve your goals. And you can do it anytime, anywhere. Simply get relaxed, comfortable, and focused. In your mind, you can write, star, and direct your own play. And whenever you need a mental boost, you can visualize your image of success. For example, if you want to be a tv anchor, visualize yourself in front of the camera delivering your message to millions of viewers.

Successful people are smart people—not necessarily book or academic smart, not even "street smart," but intuitive smart. They allow their intuition to guide them and do what feels right to them. You can also take a cue from Corporate America. Successful companies and people know who they are and are focused on what they provide. They do not try to be all things to all people, rather they find their niche and then market it like crazy. Likewise, you need to find your niche and become a marketing extraordinaire.

21st Century Worker Skill Mindset

When it comes to the 21st century world of work, chance and career opportunity favors the prepared mind. Those who are prepared for the changes in the workplace will have many more career opportunities available to them. The successful modern worker will diversify themselves and tap into many talents and technologies to keep themselves at the top of their game. They will embrace concepts such as "Me, Inc." "Free Agent," "Career Strategist," "Career Crafting," and "Doing Work that Matters."

The 21st century worker will value independent thinking, the entrepreneurial spirit, soulful work, authenticity, working in a global economy, living life on purpose, being flexible and fluid, developing multi-income sources, roles over titles, networking to find work, and using technology. There is no denying that the worker mindset is evolving to meet a new paradigm of values and economics in our society. Here are some of the different ways workers are thinking about the "new career."

➡ Has a comprehensive career/life strategy plan that includes a life vision and purpose statement, short and long-term goals, which remain flexible and open.

➡ Creates a career strategy that is flexible, and continually assesses the "fit" of the work.

➡ Sees possibilities to share knowledge, skills, and abilities in a variety of settings.

➡ Recognizes that your life's work is part of who you are (a job is something you do).

➡ Goal is to position oneself well in the constantly changing world of work.

➡ Thinks in terms of abundance—there is enough for everyone.

➡ Views oneself as a business—actively seeking out others who need your services.

➡ Thinks out of the box, knows there are many ways to do something.

➡ Develops a resume based on knowledge, skills, and abilities rather than work history alone.

➡ Learns small business skills, necessary for success as a contract worker.

➡ Recognizes that all work is meaningful and creates stepping stones to other opportunities.

➡ Knows that career development is a process that never ends.

➡ More emphasis on self-marketing (reaching out to potential customers).

➡ Has a "Can Do" attitude. Believes that even though it might be a challenge, they can make it work.

Develop Multicultural Skills

In the modern world of work, we do business within one giant global marketplace, which includes interactions and transactions with international customers and markets, both in person, via the telephone, and over the Internet. To be an effective worker in the global economy, we must become aware of how our own culture impacts us and strive to learn as much as we can about other cultures. *Culture is a way of life for a group of people, a set of rules, including laws, customs, habits, and behavior guideline. It is developed over time by a specific group (national, regional, ethnic, religious, corporate, and family), and is learned.* Put simply, culture is the software that programs the behavior of human beings. It goes without saying that there are many different kinds of cultures working together in the business world. But if we ignore our cultural differences, we will create misunderstandings and confusion. Therefore, we must make a conscious effort to raise our cultural sensitivity by raising our own self-awareness and increasing our exposure to cultures different than our own.

The term "multicultural" refers to *places and situations having people of more than one culture present.* Someone who is culturally sensitive to diverse people will be in demand in the new age of work. Multicultural skills include the ability to relate with diverse people from different backgrounds and cultures, whether they be co-workers or customers. This requires someone who is open to learn and work with people with varied experiences, values, and perspectives. Believe it or not, these skills can (and must) be learned if you set your mind to it. Some ways to develop multicultural skills include:

- Thinking globally, acting locally.
- Exposing yourself to other cultures, by reading, traveling, and interacting with multicultural people.
- Becoming literate and conversational in at least one other language.
- Taking courses and attending programs related to race, gender, or international affairs.
- Belonging to organizations and clubs whose members represent a variety of racial and ethnic backgrounds.
- Befriending someone from another country.
- Understanding that multicultural customers have different needs and expectations.

- Challenging yourself to find out more about other cultures.
- Interviewing multicultural people to find out what they think about things.
- Using good posture and acting formally, unless invited to do otherwise.
- Smiling (a smile means caring in every culture).
- Following your multicultural customer's lead—let them set the tone, pace, and style of the interaction.
- Being flexible and patient with others.

In the past, (and sometime in the present) people have mistakenly thought that anyone who was different from them was considered a threat—in other words "not good." When in reality, diversity simply means different. Different is good, it's refreshing! Thank goodness for our diversity, it makes life and work so much more interesting. Valuing diversity means understanding and appreciating that which is unique about every human being and is critical to working in our multicultural business world. When learning these skills, remember that *A mind is like a parachute, it only functions when it is open.* It is your responsibility to open yourself to learning more about how different cultures live and work.

Set Smart Goals

Whoever said, *"Prior planning prevents poor performance"* was right on the money. In the new world of work, if you don't have some sort of game plan, you will soon find yourself out of the game. So, if you want to not only stay in the game, but also win the game, you must do one better than just having a plan. You have to develop a strategy, one that includes action steps.

When there's a will, there's a way! Even underdogs can succeed, if they set their mind to it. The best way I know how to "plan your work and work your plan" is by setting goals. It is important to start thinking of your big picture first. Keep in mind what your life vision and purpose is. Once you have this in mind, you can set SMART goals, and then further break them down into specific action steps.

Remember that a goal is a dream with a deadline. Being a goal-oriented person will keep you moving forward in life. Each goal you set should be based on your overall life vision. Long-term career goals are typically 10-20 years, Mid-term goals are 4-9 years. Short-term goals are immediately-3 years.

SMART Goals

Specific: the goal is clear, you know precisely what you are going after.
Measureable: the goal is able to be measured, you will know when you have achieved it.
Achieveable: the goal is within your range, you will be able to attain it.
Reality-based: the goal is something that can be done, you will be able to do it.
Time-limited: the goal is limited to a certain time frame, you will have parameters as to when you will have completed it.

Sample Goals

<u>Goal 1:</u> To own a small business (bookstore or card shop).
Action Step—Go to Small Business Development Center and find out what resources/support are available to me.
Action Step—Seek out possible avenues through my professional network and newspaper advertisements.
Action Step—Interview friend who owns a bookstore to gain information.

<u>Goal 2:</u> To be approved for a small business loan.
Action Step—Apply to at least two financial institutions.
Action Step—Write a business plan.
Action Step—Make appointment with loan officer.

Smart Tip

➡ There may be sub-steps under each action step. For example, "Write a business plan" has several steps to it: Get sample of a business plan, write rough draft, edit rough draft, type the business plan, make final edits.

Case Illustration

Susie is a 35 year-old professional trainer wanting to make a career transition from corporate training to college teaching, which she has been thinking about doing for several years. Her passions are writing and teaching. She knows she wants to work on a college campus, and realizes that if she is going to follow her dreams, she needs to get an action plan in place before her corporate career takes her off onto another track. Since she has only earned a Bachelor's degree in English, she has to prepare to return to school to pursue her Master's and Doctorate degrees.

Once she had her long-term career objective of becoming a college English professor in mind, she was then able to set mid-term goals of visiting a local university to interview and spend time with someone doing her dream job. She also plans to become a teacher's assistant. Her short-term goals are to apply to graduate school, read several of her favorite authors, and save money for her transition from worker to student. Her list of things to do is quite long, but she feels that it will all be worth it in the end and looks forward to the challenge.

Like Susie, once you figure out what you want to do, there may be a lot of work yet to be done. You may need to acquire the necessary qualifications: *education, experience, and/or personal characteristics.* You will need to know what academic preparation or credentials are needed: a Bachelor's, Master's degree, certification, etc? What level of experience is needed? Is it an entry level, mid-level, or executive level position? What personal qualities are needed? Detail-oriented, good communication skills, etc?

From the assessment process, you should have a pretty good idea of what you bring to the table. If not, continue to raise your self-awareness of what you have to offer, and what skills you need to continue to work on. Sometimes in order to get where you want to go, you have to take a step or two "backwards." For instance, if you want to go into Human Resources but lack the qualifications, you can take a lower level administrative job, while gaining more experience, which will get "your foot in the door." Career development is no longer a linear process—you will have to be flexible and jump around to land your ideal career.

If additional education or training is necessary, where can you go to get it? Could you attend a community college or vocational training program in your community? Or would higher education or professional credentials be required? If it is experience you are lacking, there are many ways to start gaining practical experience in your field of interest. Some possibilities are:

Volunteer position—This is an unpaid position where you would be able to gain experience and make valuable contacts.

Part-time job—This is a part-time paid position where you will be able to get familiar with the work environment.

Externship—This is a short-term unpaid position, where you would spend a few days to a month following or helping out someone who is doing the kind of work you want to do.

Internship—This is a more formalized way to gain practical experience. You would spend anywhere from a few months to a year performing work for someone else. You may or may not be paid.

If you need to develop certain personal characteristics, how can you go about learning them? Perhaps by taking special training or getting mentored or coached on specific qualities. This will be the hardest area. If you really need excellent listening or communication skills, for example, to be a counselor, these are not skills you can easily pick up in a week, month, or even year of training. However, it is possible! If you really want to, you can learn anything at anytime!

Journal Assignment #21
What do you need to prepare for your chosen career field? What smart goals can you set for yourself? What steps will you take to move closer to doing your life's work?

Chapter Fifteen

The Commitment Stage

"If one advances confidently in the direction of dreams, and endeavors to live the life which he has imagined, he will meet with a success unexpected in common hours."
—Henry David Thoreau

Now that you have become prepared for your career/life's work, it is time to become committed to going after your dreams and passions. The Commitment Stage is the fourth stage in the career development process. In this chapter, you will learn how to conduct your career search, negotiate employment offers, and accept a position.

In the Commitment Stage, you will feel confident, in that you have figured out what you are meant to do. Sometimes people have known all along what they were meant to do, but were not able to commit to the process of making it happen, for whatever reason. At this stage, more than ever, you must focus your energy and keep your eye on the target.

21st Century Career Search Strategies

Job seekers often approach employers (and often the world) with a "what's in it for me" attitude. You can get a sense of their self-centeredness just by the tone of their career correspondence, particularly the cover letter, which often comes off sounding like "Please give me a job" instead of "Here's what I can do for you." As with anything, good manners go a long way. So it is important to phrase things in a more positive, giving manner. You can easily change how you come across by simply doing your research on the needs of the company or organization. This immediately shows commitment because you have taken the time to find out what they need and also how you can assist.

The truly successful job seekers approach their work and their life with "What gifts can I share?" "What can I do for you?" But especially during the job search, little things mean a lot. By doing something a little extra, you can stand out from the crowd.

The person who gets the job is the one who is best prepared and persists throughout the selection process. That means doing whatever is necessary to land your dream job or career. For the job seeker, persistence is one of the best indicators of whether or not someone will be successful. Nothing worthwhile in life comes easy. The best things in life still come from hard work and determination. The good jobs go to the ones who are willing to endure the rather cumbersome process of applying for them.

If you have looked for a job in the past year or two, you have probably learned that today's employers will make you jump through a lot of hoops to get the most basic of positions. Those who make it are the ones who proceed through each and every stage of the hiring process. More and more, companies are using applications, tests, assessments, and lengthy interviews as a way to screen people out. They know that not everyone will do everything that is asked. In fact, you can expect some pretty absurd things along the way. I had one client tell me that he applied for a job that was in California. He sent his resume and cover letter in, and received an e-mail requesting him to also send in a 15-minute video describing why he was the right person for the job. Seemingly, they were trying to save money by not having to call people or fly them out for an interview. Obviously, you have to determine how much you want a position and what you are willing to do to get it.

The job search has gotten more competitive that ever. Employers are no longer seeking just worker bees (warm bodies), they are seeking queen bees (talented minds). The search now is for "talent." Organizations want people who can think on their feet, who are problem solvers, and who can be flexible and fluid handling change.

To land your dream job, you are going to have to develop a proactive strategy. Because taking a passive approach to your job search will continue to lead you to boring, dead-end jobs where you will become disappointed quickly. Anyone can find a job, but it is much harder to create the kind of work you want. Studies have proven that the least effective way to find a job is to respond to want ads, yet this is how most people expend their time and energy during the job search. Employment agencies are also popular, but unless you are seeking temporary work or looking to gain experience, you would probably fair better on your own. Note: Some employment agencies charge a fee, while others do not.

The most effective way to find a job is through your professional network—from hearing about a job from someone. Networking, broadly defined, means talking with people who can provide a personal or professional advantage. The next most effective way is to contact the employer directly. In fact, 75% of the jobs found are through personal contacts and cold calling! And all this takes are good telephone and communication skills.

Especially in the initial process, Human Resource professionals act as gatekeepers. In fact, they screen people out of jobs, instead of referring them on (they often only refer the "most qualified" applicants to the hiring manager). If you don't get a lot of information from them, bypass them and get the name of the person who is in charge of hiring and make direct contact with him or her. If you can make personal contact with the person in charge of making the final decision, you have a much better chance of landing an interview. It is easy to get thrown out of the employment process by getting frustrated by all of the requirements. However, once you figure out what works best for *your industry,* you can make it an easy process by following the five P's of Job Searching:

Be proactive: Take charge of your job search.
Be persistent: Don't give up.
Be positive: Focus on the positive aspects of the job search and yourself.
Be productive: Develop excellent self-marketing materials.
Be patient: Believe that the right opportunity will come your way.

Job Search Smart Tips

1. Clarify your career goals.
2. Develop the education, experience, and qualities required for the desired position.
3. Tailor your resume and cover letter.
4. Identify and research potential employers.

5. Establish a network.
6. Practice your interviewing skills.
7. Keep a job search file and disk to stay organized.
8. Go on interviews and follow up.
9. Evaluate job offers.
10. Continue this process until you find the work you want to do.

A first-rate job search resembles a campaign, in that you are out there making contacts and marketing yourself. Do something positive and productive every day. You have to stay committed, especially when the going gets tough. Non-committed people have many excuses why things don't seem to be going their way. While committed people are busy making it happen. Remember, there are no hard and fast rules to the job/career search game. There are only guidelines. Sometimes breaking the rules moves you ahead, sometimes, it moves you behind. Above all, figure out what works best in your industry and do that! Strive to become a career strategist, know when to jump ship and move on and when to stay aboard.

Get Smart!
➡ If you are conducting a long-distance job search, check out the Internet for job-related sites. You can also call the Chamber of Commerce of the city and get a newcomer/jobseekers packet of information.

Case Illustration
Meredith completed her graduate degree in Counseling and began the process of looking for her first "real" professional position in her chosen career field of school counseling. Upon beginning the process, she noticed very quickly how competitive it was to land positions in the "better" school systems. The fact that most schools only had one or a few counselors meant that unless someone retired or left a position, there were very few new positions. In addition to having to fill out extensive application materials, sending out numerous resumes and cover letters/references, the interview process was long and drawn out. Sometimes she would not hear from anyone for months, and often rarely received a letter of confirmation or rejection. She talked with others in her field and they were experiencing the same thing, so she knew it wasn't that she didn't have the necessary quali-

fications. It was just that it was going to take some time to find the right fit.

Despite the obvious challenges, she persisted and finally had three solid interviews. Two were with school systems more than 40 miles from where she lived, and the other was with a local school. She did not receive an offer from the local system, but did receive an offer from both of the other systems. After evaluating each offer and the school culture, she chose the one where she would be counseling students who were very different from her cultural background. At this school, 90% of the students she would be counseling were from a very different ethnic and economic background than her own. Meredith felt like this would be the best fit for her and excitedly accepted the position.

Top Ten Mistakes Job Seekers Make

If you are like me, you may wonder how we have such high turn-over rates in today's job market? It is due to not only a good economy, but also because people are not doing enough assessment and investigation before conducting their job search. An employment *mis-match* occurs when you have not done enough soul-searching to know what kind of work you are interested in, what kind of environment you would feel comfortable, etc. The result is job jumping, which is a great expense in time and energy. This can become a deadly cycle and is just not smart. If you are committed to winning the career search game, then you will be committed to learn from other people's mistakes. Here is a short list of the top ten mistakes job seekers make. Read them and learn, so you can save yourself a lot of time and energy.

1) *Not knowing the kind of job that would be a good fit for you.*
You must spend a good amount of time figuring out who you are and what you have to offer an employer, before you can begin the job search process.

2) *Plunging in to the search with no prior planning/strategizing.*
People wear themselves out by applying for every job they come across, giving little thought to whether they would even want to do it or not.

3) *Failing to research likely employers.*
Target your job search campaign to employers/customers who are look-

ing for someone with your skills and qualities.

4) *Relying on traditional methods of job searching.*
Use all of the options available to you, including the Internet and networking. Do not rely on one or two ways of looking for a job, such as the want ads or temporary agencies. Use a variety to find out what works best for you.

5) *Not being organized.*
Keep a job search file, with copies of everything (letters, notes, information about the company, etc.). You will find it helpful to refer to again and again. Have one disk on which you put all your job search materials. (Have a back up file saved).

6) *Being lazy.*
Don't just sit around waiting for the telephone to ring. You have to get out and beat the bushes every day. Looking for a job is a full-time job. You should be spending at least 20-30 hours a week on your job search.

7) *Paying a resume service to write your resume for you.*
If you are going to pay someone, pay them to teach you how and why to write a quality resume—you need to know how to do this for yourself!

8) *Not involving others in your search.*
The more people who know that you are looking for work, the better. You never know who in your network of friends, family, and colleagues can lead you to your next position.

9). *Poor interviewing skills.*
The interview is your final exam. If you do not pass with flying colors, you will not get the job. Interview skills can be learned. If you practice them, you will improve.

10) *Not following directions.*
Do what the employer asks. If they ask you to fill out the application with blue ink, do it. If they ask you to take a test, do it. Many of the things they have you do are ways to see who has the persistence and stamina to do what is required.

Smart Tip
➡ Job seeker survival skills include career focus and personal determination.

Evaluate Your Employment Offers

Once you have been offered a job or position that you are interested in, you must evaluate whether or not it would be a good fit for you. Rate your job offer(s) on this scale.

1= Poor   2=Average   3=Good   4=Excellent   N/A

Benefit Package   _____
Company size & style   _____
Co-Workers   _____
Career fit   _____
Challenge   _____
Interest & variety   _____
Supervisor   _____
Salary   _____
Relevant to career goals   _____
Location   _____
Responsibilities   _____
Personal Satisfaction   _____
Professional Development   _____
Reputation of Employer   _____
Travel   _____

Total   _____

Your Score
60-54:   Excellent Offer
53-46:   Good Offer
45-39:   Average Offer
38 or below: Poor Offer
One positive aspect of this offer
is_____

One negative aspect of this offer
is_____

When evaluating an employment offer, there are a couple of other things besides salary to consider: the benefits package and the organizational culture of the place you will be working. Carefully look at what kind of benefits the company is offering you, because sometimes, a great benefit package can make up for a lower salary. Pay attention to benefits like health/life insurance, 401K, stock options, childcare, employee assistance programs, flextime, retirement benefits, tuition reimbursement, and wellness programs.

Being happy in your work environment is becoming an increasingly important whole life consideration. Corporate culture can be as unhealthy as a dysfunctional family. And since you will be spending even more time with your co-workers than your own family, I think it is important to find out before hand, (as much as possible) if your values are in line with the organization's. Far too many people have learned the hard way that money and prestige are poor substitutes for inner peace and a sense of meaning. Sure you may be making $60,000 a year, but will your soul suffer because of it?

Here are some questions to consider regarding organizational culture:
What is the organizational climate of the place where you intend to work?
What behaviors are rewarded?
How is loyalty defined?
How does the company deal with change?
What are the organizational values?
Do they abide by their mission?
Will you fit in? Do you want to fit in? Or would you have to change yourself too much?
Can you be "Who you really are?"

Negotiate Your Offer

A Chinese proverb says it best: *"To guess is cheap. To guess wrong is expensive."* In regards to the job market, you will make what you expect to make. What you expect to make is often tied to how much you think you are worth. So the first thing you need to do before you get to the negotiating table is to develop a realistic (but optimistic) idea of your market worth. Going in with an amount in mind will help you to emerge with a better deal. Like anything else in an economically-motivated society, you are a commodity, so start thinking as such. To research your market value (the going rate for people in your industry with skills similar to yours), visit www.jobsmart.org or http://stats.bls.gov

The goal is to have the offer directly linked to the work that you will perform and how the value of said work will impact the company's operations. So even if your past jobs paid considerably less than what you hope to make, you can still get paid what you are worth. When you negotiate, there are a couple of rules to keep in mind. The first is to know what you want and what you are willing to accept. Being clear on what you are after makes all the difference in the world. The second is to feel the other side out—how bad do you think they want you, what is the salary range, and what are they willing to offer?

The third is to let them speak first. When an offer is extended, if they ask you "What were you hoping to make?" Instead of saying: "forty thousand," say, "What have you budgeted for this position?" (or something similar). This way, you will not over-cut or under-cut yourself. And you have put the ball in their court. You want them to state the salary figure first. From there, you can start the negotiations.

Keep in mind that you will want to look at the entire offer, as some aspects other than salary may be negotiable, such as paid professional development or extra time off. However, you should get a pretty clear idea of how flexible they are about salary just by the way they say it. If you get a sense that there is room to grow, then don't be afraid to ask for more. For example, if they say, the position pays $40,000 depending on experience, then say, "Well, as you know I bring ten years experience in this area and expect to make in the range of $42,000-$44,000, based on the duties of the job."

If salary comes up too early in the conversation, say something like, "Can we come back to that when you have a better picture of what I have to offer?" or, "I would rather discuss all aspects of the position before looking at salary issues."

Accept the Position

When they call you to make the offer, always say that you need at least a day to think it over and that you will get back to them at a certain time. This is standard operating procedure, and you may even need to take longer if you are a hot commodity and/or looking at several offers.

You can accept the position in person, on the phone, in writing, or a combination of ways. If you decide to put it in writing, look back at the chapter on career correspondence for a sample acceptance letter.

When you accept a position, contract, or project, you should feel good about it. It should be something you want to do and will feel good about doing. If you are not 100% sure about it, you may want to stop and consider whether accepting it is the right thing to do. Many times our intuition tells us what positions are right and what positions aren't, but we don't pay attention to the signals.

Of course, if it is the right thing to do, you will feel a mixture of anxiety and excitement at the prospect of getting started.

Journal Assignment #22
What job search mistakes have you made in the past? What can you do to further commit to your chosen career field? What can you do to improve your negotiation skills?

Chapter Sixteen

The Retention Stage

*"Doing your best at this moment places you in the best position
for your next moment in life."*
—Oprah Winfrey

You are now successfully established in your career field. Is it time to
kick back and relax? Not if you want to stay employed. The Retention
Stage is the fifth stage in the career development process. In this chapter, you will learn how to present a positive image, use excellent communication skills, provide first-class customer service skills, and cultivate a professional network.

In the Retention Stage, you will feel comfortable in your career
field, as you will now have figured out how things work in your industry. You will want to remain committed to your career by continually
updating your skill set and staying current with industry standards.

Present a Positive Image
Getting a good job is only half the battle. You must also keep it. Your
image, communication, and customer service skills will play a big part
in your ability to stay gainfully employed. What does a professional
look like in the modern world of work? A 21st century professional will
be someone who presents a positive image, has high work ethics, and
strives for excellence in their work. Professionalism in the modern era
will come down to having your words and actions match each other.
Thus, trust and character will become important to your job retention.

Your image is made up by your attitude, your appearance, and your communication style. Appearance consists of the way you present yourself visually to others—through your particular fashion style, your inner energy, and your body language.

They say, "attitude is everything." This is because no matter what you do or say, your attitude shows. Of course, developing a positive outlook, being open, and focusing on what is right with the world will go a long way in helping you build a polished image.

Your particular communication style is made up of both your verbal and non-verbal behaviors. The way you speak and carry yourself says a lot about you. Be sure to be articulate, open, and an especially good listener.

Presenting a positive image opens the doors of opportunity. Now, we all know that it is sometimes hard to tell who the best worker will be. But if you are the one sending the message to others that you are a qualified, competent, and caring employee simply by the image that you present, then you will be the one who will likely be presented with more advancement opportunities. A simple image check is when you get dressed for work, stop and think, *Is this what I want to say about myself today?*

Having a solid set of work ethics will help you to act the part of a professional. If you are in a work or life situation where your values are challenged, you must make a choice: either compromise your ethics and keep the job or stand by your ethics and perhaps risk losing a job, a title, or prestige. Throughout time, it has never been easy to always do the right thing. But now more than ever, it is important for people to stand up for what they believe to be right.

Ethics are a set of moral principles or values that governs an individual or group.
Ethical means conforming to an accepted professional standard of conduct.
Integrity is the firm adherence to a code of values.
Moral means conforming to a standard of right behavior.
Professionalism is adherence to standards established either formally or informally by tradition and members of a profession.

The first step in honoring your ethics is to know your ethical value system. Then you must understand how your values fit in with those of the situation, recognize when your values are called into question, and finally make a decision when the need arises. I truly believe that when more people in business begin standing up for what is right, we will reinvent the work that we do and lead our society back to a more ethical, sane, and safe way of life.

Professionalism and ethics are not limited to executive level positions. In fact, you can be a very professional and ethical waitress or window cleaner. As long as you give it your best, maintain a sense of pride in your work, and follow your inner self.

To retain your job, you also need to continually find ways to add value. Your company or clients will take care of you as long as you bring value to the work that you do. People who add value will always find work because they are always coming up with bright ideas and innovations to do the job better and more efficiently. Become an idea-factory. Everyone has good ideas every day, the only difference is that some people actually act on them!

Become a change agent, someone who is on the lookout for new and better ways to do the job. Being open to change will keep you excited about your job. As you initiate and implement change, you continue to be challenged. How do you get re-charged in your work— by continually striving for excellence, and moving out of your comfort zone every now and then. In fact, get comfortable with being *uncomfortable*. Realize that you will only be employed if you are actively contributing. You will have no choice but to stay fresh, and avoid becoming stale and/or burned out. There are many folks who just stay too long in their job and simply can't be as effective as they were ten or fifteen years earlier. For instance, I think *all* politicians should have term limits. Obviously someone who has been in office for 20 or 30 years and still doing things the way he always did, cannot be good for the public he serves. Most people (not just politicians) lose their luster and ability to produce at "star level" when they have been doing the same thing for too many years.

Smart Tip
➡ Simultaneously pursue employment and education to keep abreast of trends in your field.

Get Smart!
➡ If you want to be promoted, look, act, and talk the part of that position.

Case Illustration

Darlene is an out-going female in her late forties. She returned to her home state of Georgia after a ten-year hiatus and found herself looking for work related to her interest in counseling and helping people develop professionally. She was very clear on the kind of work she wanted to do and began looking for and found her current position five years ago. As part of the Continuing Education department at a major university, she began coordinating programs and courses. Since then she has re-created her position to fit in with her career needs and professional strengths. She has developed and presented a very successful professional national curriculum to help employees who work at various state agencies learn and grow professionally. The program has been so well received in Georgia that it has been expanded and classes are now being offered at locations throughout the southeastern United States.

Darlene's program is in high demand and has even received an Award of Recognition from the university. There is no doubt that she continues to be challenged and fully engaged in her work, because she continually finds new ways to apply her skills and talents. She has certainly carved out a place for herself in her profession that is meaningful both to her and the people she serves.

Provide First-Class Customer Service

Do you ever wonder why there is so much bad customer service? I believe the reason is two-fold. First, people are disconnected from their inner selves. Secondly, they are performing work that holds little or no meaning for them. With our heavy reliance on technology and machines, people are actually modeling machine-like, impersonal behavior. It's as though we have become industrialized in our hearts, and thus unable to respond from our true Spirit.

Everyone works in customer service. No matter what field you are in the modern world of work, you will be serving customers (whether it is directly or indirectly). So, you may as well get smart and get good at it! In order to better serve them, you must listen and respond to their needs. Customer service comes down to how well you treat and serve people. First-class customer service means not just meeting someone's expectations, but going the extra mile to make that person feel special.

You know great service when you see or experience it. The person's words are friendly and courteous, their actions, thoughtful and appropriate. First-class customer service can (and must) be developed. You can begin by practicing care and concern for your customers, both the internal (those you work with) and the external (those you work for), and then working hard at knowing your job inside and out.

There are two dimensions to customer service: the personal side (relating to people) and the procedural side (technical know-how of the job you perform). If you become highly skilled at both sides of service, you will always enjoy your work, no matter what setting you find yourself in.

If you take notice of your customer needs as they change, you can change your service to meet their needs. First-class service providers pay close attention to what employers and customers are looking for, and respond accordingly. Attitude and aptitude are equally important when serving customers. If you are very good at the procedures of the job, but treat people impersonally, they will elect to do their business elsewhere. Likewise, if you are friendly, but are unable to assist the customer in his or her problem, they too will take their business somewhere else.

Determine Your Customer's Expectations

Customers have five basic expectations: Receiving *Attention, Respect, Understanding, Information, and Results.* Attention, Respect, and Understanding fall into the personal category of service. Information and Results fall into the procedural category of service.
Strive to delight them on both sides and you will no doubt be a success.

Unmet expectations: You do not meet the bare minimum of customer's expectations. They will not return to your business.
Meet expectations: You meet the bare minimum of customer's expectations. They may or may not return to your business.
Exceed expectations: You exceed the customer's expectations. They may or may not return to your business.
Delight them! You go above and beyond the call of duty. They will definitely keep returning to your business!
Example: you own a bed and breakfast. A couple makes a reservation

for this coming weekend. If you *do not meet* the customer's expectations, the room would not be sufficient or ready as requested. The unsatisfied customer will likely tell ten or more people about their negative experience. If you *just meet* their expectations by providing a clean room and courteous service, they may come back (or not). If you *exceed* their expectations by providing a well-decorated, clean, comfortable room, courteous service, and a complimentary continental breakfast, they may come back. But if you *absolutely delight* them with a beautiful, clean, spacious room, extra courteous and attentive service, and a delicious full breakfast delivered to their room, they will return and probably will tell ten or more people about their wonderful experience.

As we all know, word-of-mouth is the best form of advertising. If you delight just ten customers, you will likely have at least return visits from them, plus another 100 to 200 more guests staying at your bed and breakfast!

Treat Selling as a Service

Just like everyone is in "customer service," we all perform some level of sales. When I teach customer service skills, it encompasses two premises. (1) Selling goes hand-in-hand with customer service and (2) Customers hate to be sold to, but they love to buy!
Selling is a service in which you provide to your customers, where you act as a consultant to help them make an educated decision. Again, combining skills in both dimensions of service: the personal and procedural. Effective selling involves listening to the customer and finding out what their needs are, so that you can offer them possible solutions. A good salesperson will sound more like a helpful neighbor than someone selling your something.

In reality, you are always selling, whether it is a product, a program, or yourself. So, you may as well get good at it. The "hard-sell" is out. The "soft-sell" is in. A soft sell is where you *lead* the customer to a make a decision.

LEAD stands for: Listen to the customer.

Encourage the customer's participation.

Act to meet their needs.

Decide if they are satisfied.

If their response is "yes," then personalize the closing and invite them to come again. If "no," then go back to the first step of Listening. It is also helpful to know how the selling cycle works:

Build Rapport: Welcome the customer and make them feel comfortable.
Identify Needs: Ask questions to determine needs.
Provide Solutions: Offer two or three solutions based on their needs.
Sell Benefits: Highlight the benefits of the product or service.
Value-Added Features: Suggest a complementary product or feature to go with the item.
Close the Sale: Guide them to a conclusion in a direct or indirect way. For example, a direct close: "Would you like for me to reserve the weekend of the 28th for you on your credit card?" Or an indirect close: "I can hold your reservation for 24 hours, would you like me to do that now?"

Smart Tip
➡ Always personalize your customer interactions, by calling the person by their name and offering them your business card or telephone number.

Use Excellent Communication Skills

In the world of work, from getting the job to keeping the job, effective communication skills are essential. Interpersonal communication can be defined as *the exchange of information through verbal and non-verbal means to one or more people.* In order for a message to be accurately sent to another person, a two-way process must occur. One person must send a message, and another must receive it. The only way to be sure if the message intended to be sent was the one the other person actually heard, is through feedback. Feedback provides people with specific information, usually in terms of feelings and perceptions, about how their words and/or actions were received. When feedback is delivered in a positive and supportive manner, interpersonal improvement becomes possible. Many business experts agree that effective communication between employees is the foundation on which teamwork and cooperation is built.

Interpersonal communication is a complicated process because each of us has our own unique perceptions and interpretations of any given statement or situation. Oftentimes, messages are interpreted differently than how we intended them to be. When messages get lost, mixed-up, or are not heard by the receiver, *mis-communication* occurs. In order to help eliminate the possibility of mis-communication, it is important to become aware of your own particular communication style. There are three styles of communication: *passive, aggressive, assertive*. They are formed from two basic approaches: directness and responsiveness.

Directness represents the amount of effort a person uses to influence other people's thoughts or actions. Those who are direct in their communication style are loud, outspoken, use direct statements, give opinions, and tend to be risk-takers. Those who are indirect in their communication style are soft-spoken, ask a lot of questions, withhold opinions, and tend to speak cautiously (they think before they speak).

Responsiveness represents the amount of emotion a person expresses to others. Those who respond to others with control are task-oriented, show little emotion, are conservative in dress and manner, and use subdued gestures. Those who respond to others with high emotion are relationship-oriented, show a lot of emotion, are informal in dress and manner, and use dramatic gestures.

Passive: This person does not openly share his or her thoughts and feelings. She/he chooses to hold strong thoughts or feelings in.

Aggressive: This person harshly shares his or her thoughts and feelings. She/he tends to overpower others with his or her words.

Assertive: This person appropriately shares his or her thoughts and feelings. She/he has a healthy balance when displaying emotion and directness.

To find out which style you are, ask yourself what would you do or say if you had a disagreement with a co-worker about something that was very important to you?

In interpersonal communication, there are two elements that are even more important to the interpretation than the actual words you say: *how you say it and your body language.* If what you say is not perceived as believable or is in direct contradiction to what your body is saying, the person will have difficulty figuring out what you mean. To be sure you are sending the message you intended to send, balance what you say with how you say it, and be conscious of your non-verbal communication. It is also very important to be a flexible communicator. You can do this by being versatile. Versatility is the ability to adapt to each person and situation, so that you can connect with him or her based on his or her communication style. If you don't believe that you can become a versatile communicator, take a moment to write your signature with your dominant hand. Now, write it with your non-dominant hand. You should discover that you *can* write it with both hands, although one will look better than the other. However, if you practiced writing with your non-dominant hand long enough, your writing style would improve. Likewise, you can become versatile with your communication style. You just need the practice.

Get Smart!
➡ The key to becoming a good communicator is to tune in to your particular communication style, become more assertive, be aware of incongruencies in your delivery, and strive for versatility.

Become an Active Listener

Hearing is a biological function, most people can hear unless they are hearing impaired. Listening, however, is a skill which takes active participation and conscious effort. Listening takes the words and sounds that we hear and interprets them. The importance of active listening cannot be overstated. In order to be effective on the job (and in life), you must develop your listening skills. This means being actively engaged with the person speaking by looking at them, asking questions, and reflecting back to them what you heard them say.

There are three main elements to active listening: *tuning-in, asking questions, and reflecting on what the person has said.* Tuning in means being fully present with the person and eliminating internal or external distractions. Asking questions involves posing thoughtful, relevant questions to further understand the other person's feelings or thoughts. And reflecting involves repeating back to them in your own words the facts, feelings, and underlying meaning of the words.

There are many benefits to becoming a good listener: better ability to help others, social acceptance and popularity, and the ability to avoid problems that result from a lack of listening. To listen more effectively, clear your mind, maintain an open body stance and good eye contact, pay attention to not only the logical content of the message, but also the emotional, and respond appropriately (by nodding, smiling, or asking a probing question).

Are You a Good Listener?

Answer each question Yes or No.

1. I am able to empathize with other people's situations.
2. I avoid interrupting other people when they are speaking.
3. I avoid thinking of how I am going to respond to the conversation while someone is speaking.
4. I give people my full attention when speaking with them.
5. I do not try to tell "my story" as soon as someone tells me their story.
6. I avoid thinking I know what the speaker is about to say.
7. I maintain good eye contact and body language when speaking with someone.
8. I ask a lot of questions when someone is talking with me.
9. I reflect back feelings and facts, so I am sure I heard the person correctly.
10. People often come to me just to talk.

If you answered "Yes" to seven or more questions, you are a good listener. If you answered "No" to five or more, you may need to work on your listening skills.

Get Smart!

➡ Listening is one of the most powerful communication tools we have available in our work toolbox.

Watch Your Non-Verbal Communication

What is your body language saying about you? What subtle signals are you sending out to the world via your posture, gestures, or touch? Albert Mehrabian, a UCLA researcher said that as much as 55% of the message communicated is from "body language," while 38% of the message communicated comes from how the words are spoken, and a mere 7% of the message communicated is from the *actual words spo-*

ken. Thus, our non-verbal communication needs to be monitored as much as our verbal communication. Particularly with lying or deception, non-verbal cues (body language and facial expressions) are more accurate and easier to interpret than what the person is saying. Have you ever thought about what your body language says about you?

Are you communicating openness or defensiveness?

Honesty or deceit?

Happiness or sadness?

Trust or mistrust?

Confidence or insecurity?

Aggressiveness or passiveness?

Warmth or indifference?

Love or hate?

Do you smile at people a lot?

Do you tend to touch people when you talk?

Do you walk fast or slow?

Do you use hand gestures when telling a story?

Do you nod your head in agreement when someone is talking?

Do you face other people when having a serious conversation?

Do you feel comfortable maintaining eye contact for more than a few seconds at a time?

Do you offer a firm, confident handshake?

Do you wear outfits appropriate for the situation?

We all talk with our bodies every day and don't even realize it because it is so natural. So, we must become aware that our bodies may be sending out mixed or altogether inaccurate signals. If you want to make a good first impression on an interview for example, you don't show up wearing an outfit that you'd would wear on a Sunday afternoon while washing the car. You would not look away from the person or look down at your feet while talking. You would want to put your "best face" forward—smile and talk with confidence, look attractive, and make a concerted effort to show interest in the interviewer by leaning slightly forward in your chair.

Job Retention Smart Tips

Listening

- When you are not sure about something that is said or done, be sure to ask for clarification.
- Don't do all the talking. Strive for 60-70% listening, 30-40% talking while on the job.
- Don't interrupt. Allow adequate time for the person to answer or ask a question.
- Keep your emotions in check. An angry person does not listen well.
- Take time to tune in, reflect back, and ask questions of the other person.
- Maintain good eye contact and an open-mind.
- Try being a counselor for a day. Let a friend or co-worker talk out a problem and listen without judgment or giving advice.

Relating

- Establish positive relationships with your boss, know his or her strengths/weaknesses, and preferred communication style (in person or in writing).
- Find a mentor to look up to.
- Value diversity and learn from others.
- Accept constructive criticism and learn from mistakes.
- Surround yourself with people who bring out the best in you.
- Avoid getting caught up in office gossip and politicking.

Writing

- Be brief and to the point in all your business correspondence.
- Introduce one thought per paragraph.
- Read books and magazines in your career field to see what is being researched and written about.
- Use an active rather than passive voice.
- Organize your thoughts with an outline before you begin writing.
- Consider how your message will affect your readers.
- Keep your messages concise and avoid sending emotionally-charged messages.

Speaking
- Speak confidently and directly.
- If asked to give a presentation, rehearse your material and use visual aids to support your ideas.
- Maintain good eye contact and body language with your audience.
- Don't preach or try to convince people of your beliefs. Simply state them with conviction and confidence.
- Whenever possible, ask a lot of questions.
- Use paraphrasing (restating what the person has said).
- Give speeches, this will show you how to effectively organize and deliver your message.

Working
- Learn something new every day.
- Ask questions about your job.
- Look for ways you "can do" it.
- Provide solutions and suggestions, not problems and complaints.
- Constantly re-invent yourself.
- Choose a goal, then walk like, walk like, look like, think like, act like and be like it.

A word about the use of e-mail. E-mail is a faster medium than conventional pen and paper. It produces an instant message. It also is a disposable communication—people usually delete it after reading it. Therefore, if you have something important to say, and/or want the message to last, then you should write it the old-fashioned way (memo or letter).

Cultivate a Network

Cultivating a professional network is critical to staying employed. Career success and strategizing is directly related to visible and invisible connections, commonly referred to as networks. A network is much like a spider web in that it keeps growing with every contact you make. It's been said before that it's not what you know, but *who* you know. In the modern world of work, networking has gone a step further—it is not only who you know, but who knows you (and your work). Networking is *the process through which people within a system help the advancement of others by sharing information, giving support, and strategic positioning.* In order to maintain your marketability, you must think of your career as a business, one that includes the functions of planning, research and development, operations, information systems, sales, public relations, finance, and interpersonal skills.

The purpose of networking is to stay connected to people in your field who can help you advance and recommend you for positions. When you are networking, you can develop relationships with others in person and online—either way gives you the opportunity to meet and connect.

The types of networks you develop can expand your sphere of influence and help you get from one place to another more easily. Your contact network is everyone you know, and have connection to. These are not only people who can hire you, but who can get you in touch with others by providing information about opportunities. Everyone has contacts, but they don't become beneficial until you start to call on them.

Make a list of your contacts: family, friends, neighbors, alumni, past employers or coworkers, church and community organizations, social organizations, anyone who has expressed an interest in your success. Include their name, organization, relation to you, telephone number, address, and e-mail and put it in your contact system.

When making contact, whether by telephone, letter, e-mail, fax, or in person, share your current projects and plans for the future with them. You never know to whom or where they will refer you to for additional help. Your career network is a specific group designed for career networking, such as a women's career group. Some of these networks are loosely based, others are more formal. Some have membership dues, others don't. Professional career networks are usually found in larger cities.

Smart Tip
➡ Develop a record keeping or card file system for keeping track of each contact made, whether you use a Rolodex or a computer system log book, etc.

Another way to cultivate your network is by becoming and staying actively involved in professional associations/organizations. No matter what your career interests, there is a group or association for you to join. There are thousands of such organizations across the country, and many that are industry or trade specific. Research them, and join the ones you feel you can get the most out of. Membership in professional associations gives you access to informal and formal contacts where you can form a mutually beneficial relationship with like-minded individuals. Check your local paper for meeting times and topics. And, of course, there is Internet networking, such as chat rooms and list services. This is a great way to keep abreast of trends and to learn about benchmarking in your career field.

Get Smart!
➡ Reciprocity is the name of networking. Offer your help, assistance, and appreciation often. Be courteous and professional at all times. Follow up with leads given to you, provide feedback, and always thank your source.

Journal Assignment #23
What are your five best image assets? What areas could use some improvement? What are some work retention ideas you can implement? How can you further develop your network?

Chapter Seventeen

The Transition Stage

"Not in his goals, but his transitions, man is great."
—Ralph Waldo Emerson

If you are like most people, you will experience several career transitions throughout your lifetime. The key is to become comfortable, and to learn to apply your skill set to a new career field. The Transition Stage is about knowing when to make career changes, developing resiliency, and adjusting to a new work environment.

The Transition Stage is characterized by feelings of dis-comfort, in that you are unsure of what you will be doing next (and/or if you will be happy). In this stage, you will learn to make conscious changes in your career direction.

How Satisfied Are You in Your Current Position?

A transition can be defined as *passing from one place, state, or condition to another.* The key to making successful career transitions is to know when to move on, exit gracefully, and have a support group. Knowing when to stay and when to go will help you make easier career transitions. Burn-out is one of the major causes of work-related stress. Knowing your signs and developing a strategy to cope before you reach the burn-out stage is crucial to helping you make career transitions. Keeping a fresh perspective allows you to avoid burn-out (too much stress) or boredom (not enough stress).

Answer the following with a Yes or No

1. You feel proud to do what you do where you
are currently employed. _____
2. You feel an appropriate level of challenge
and comfort at your current position. _____
3. You enjoy going to work every day. _____
4. You are receiving adequate compensation
and appreciation at your job. _____
5. Your values are compatible with the organization's. _____
6. Your work allows you to pursue personal
interests and hobbies. _____
7. Your knowledge, skills, and abilities are
being fully utilized on the job. _____
8. You feel that you are a making a contribution
to society through the work that you perform. _____
9. You are comfortable with the location and
environment and culture of the
place where you work. _____
10. You often tell friends and family about the
good things that happened to you during the day. _____
11. You rarely have thoughts of
"take this job and shove it." _____
12. You seldom feel the need to look
for another job. _____
13. You are rarely irritable and impatient at work. _____
14. You feel appreciated at your job. _____

Get Smart!

➡ If you answered:
11 or more with Yes: You are satisfied with your current position.
7-10 with Yes: You are in a state of flux and could go either way,
but probably leaning towards dissatisfaction.
5 or less with Yes: You are likely dissatisfied.

Count on Career Change

When it comes to our career, the only thing we all can count on is change. However, like I said before, we don't really change careers (we have only one career in a lifetime) as much as we change occupations.

No one is immune to changing occupational directions. Professionals, non-professionals, business executives, teachers, and even rock stars have to change career fields at some point in their life. In fact, there are outplacement services for doctors and lawyers. As the needs of society change, we have to continuously find new ways to apply our skills.

Career experts have predicted that the average worker will have several very different occupations in a lifetime. The key is to transfer skills from one position to the next and to continue to build on your repertoire. The real trick to career changing is to have as much control over it as possible. Arguably, the most famous career changer in the last several decades was Ronald Reagan, who went from being a movie star, to president of a union, to regent of a university, to governor of a state, to president of the United States.

As with any change, it comes by taking a risk and mustering up courage. The quote that comes to mind: *You cannot discover a new ocean unless you have the courage to lose sight of the shore."* Challenging yourself to explore unchartered waters can be very rewarding. If you can break out of you career comfort zone and try on a new outfit, a new job or career, you can discover a whole new world.

How can you become motivated to change? Look at yourself in the mirror and make an honest assessment of yourself. Do you like who you see? If not, what can you do about it? You must first like and respect yourself, and deem yourself worthy of something better in order to make a major life change. And then you just have to do it!

If you begin by having the belief that you are where you need to be, experiencing what you need to be experiencing, making a change will be easier. But if you hold on too tightly to a job (or anything else for that matter) you miss valuable opportunities that could be better suited to you. Expending too much energy resisting change goes against the natural order of the universe. The very essence of life is change. Instead of rooting down like a oak tree, bend like a willow, flow with the winds of change.

There are two kinds of change: voluntary and involuntary. Obviously, the voluntary kind is easier to handle, because we choose it. The involuntary kind is more difficult to handle because it comes from someone else or some situation we did not choose. The Serenity Prayer is good to keep in mind when going through a difficult change: *"God grant me the serenity to accept the things I cannot change, to change the things I can, and the wisdom to know the difference."* It is true that you can have change without improvement. But it is nearly impossible to have improvement without change. In other words, to improve, we must change. Change can be very good for us.

However, most of us want to be in as much control over our lives as possible. Ideally, in order to make smart decisions, we will strive to make more self-imposed changes. Life will usually provide you with signs, but you have to pay attention and follow your path where ever it may lead you. In terms of career development, making the changes that you want when you want will lead to much easier career transitions. As with anything, you have a choice as to how you deal with your changes. Sometime dealing with them immediately works best. Sometimes waiting to gain more information works best. Also, the extent and timing of the change can affect your equilibrium. If you stay in the same field and just change employers, that is fairly stressful, but manageable. If you decide to make a complete career overhaul, and find that what you really need to do is return to school and finish your degree, then you need to be very well-prepared for that change. According to *Workforce in Transition*, there are some common reactions to transitions: disbelief and denial, acknowledgement of feeling, physical and mental distress, confusion and panic, anger and hostility, renewed hope and rebuilding. Depending on the kind of change you are undergoing, you will feel differently and move through each stage at varying rates.

Case Illustrations

Bill was a successful optometrist for twenty-two years when he decided to make a major career change. He had enjoyed the ability to educate his customers about eye care and treatment for problems, but had come to a place in his career where he wanted a new challenge. He had taken a course or two in computer programming at the local community college and had developed an interest in computer technology. As a result, he decided to go back to school for a Bachelor's degree in information technology. He went to school at night, and continued to work full-time. While completing his program, he would often help other students who were having trouble. He was asked to be a lab assistant on the weekends. After completing his program, he discovered that he had a passion for teaching the subject and ended up getting a job with the college that he attended.
Melvin was a professional football player for five years until he suffered a

shoulder injury that resulted in his early retirement from the game. Since he was very involved in volunteer activities in his community, he was quite well known in his hometown. A few years ago he was offered a position as Director of the Fatherhood Initiative for the state of Florida. In his role, he works with fathers and families to help them have a more meaningful connection. He is very dedicated to his position and feels as if he has found his true mission in life.

Involuntary Termination

Everyone should be fired or laid off at least once in their life. It builds character. And if you believe as I do, that everything happens for a reason, then you can come to terms with the situation and move on. If you are laid off or fired, don't do anything at first. Give yourself time to just *be.* You don't need to immediately start sending out resumes. What you need to do is to take a moment to breathe. Feel your feelings of anger and frustration, but don't fall into the victim mode. Accept the situation and then begin to take small steps to get back on track. To begin with, keep a daily routine. Get up early and have a plan for the day. Find ways to fill your time besides just job-searching. Exercise, do jobs around the house, and find meaning in the transition so you can bring closure to it.

Next, view this turn of events as an opportunity to take stock of your life. In fact, what an opportunity to re-evaluate where you are with your career and what direction you would like to go in next. If you find that you need additional help or guidance, do not hesitate to meet with a career development professional, they can help you assess and redirect.

They say that whatever doesn't kill you will make you stronger. Losing a job can produce significant financial stress and emotional duress. Deal with the stress, handle your emotions, and manage the change that you are undergoing. Keep your perspective. After all, your job was just one part of your very full, abundant life. Remember that when one door shuts, another opens. Unfortunately, we often look so longingly at the one that just closed, we neglect to see the many that may have opened. Finding ways to adjust to your new life situation is essential.

Adjustment Process

Shock

You are not fully aware of what has happened.

Resistance

Your may be in denial or try to place blame on others.

> Stages of resistance: *Relief* (you feel as if a burden has been lifted and begin to see opportunity).
>
> *Anger* (you blame those you might think are responsible).
>
> *Depression* (you may feel depressed once the reality of the situation sets in).

Exploration

You start to explore other options.

Acceptance

You come to terms with the situation and gain the energy and desire to move forward.

Action

You start to take action on specific goals or plans.

Change happens to all of us, but everyone handles it differently. There are some common feelings that are associated with sudden changes: you may feel awkward, uneasy, annoyed, frustrated, unsure of yourself, and alone. When you start to feel overwhelmed, take time to reflect and refocus. Know your vision and your values, set realistic goals, and learn from setbacks. Some grieving is natural, but the faster you can move through the process, the better. You may feel an initial loss of identity (Americans identify very strongly with the work we do). And you may mourn the loss of your network (the social life that was linked to your job). You may not know quite what to do with yourself (as you were not ready to be unemployed). But there are some ways to cope. First, it important to understand what happened, accept the situation, change what you can, and brainstorm your options. Then you can begin again.

Problem-Solving Model

Define the problem.

Investigate it in detail.

Produce potential solutions.
Select the best.
Try it out.
Evaluate the results.

Manage Career Change
- Remember change has many positive benefits.
- Focus on what is to be gained.
- Join a support group.
- Get professional help, if necessary.
- Set priorities and goals.
- Practice stress-reducing techniques.
- Talk about things with someone you trust.
- Concentrate on what you did right on your last job.
- Remember your contributions.
- Update your resume.
- List your positive work-related attributes.
- Be aware of your strengths and weaknesses.
- Ask yourself what can be learned from the situation.
- Volunteer or spend time doing things you always wanted to do, but never had the time or energy for.
- Think creatively about possible career/life directions you can take.

Develop Resiliency
The #1 skill to develop in today's world of work is resiliency, or the ability to "bounce back." Resiliency will enable you to more easily handle all kinds of life transitions.

Resilient Qualities:
Interconnected to others: Has a keen sense of the inter-connectedness of all life
Driven by values: Makes decisions from personal value system.
Require solitude: Takes time to reflect.
Self-reliant: Knows that they are responsible for their own life.
Is creative and playful: Able to have fun and be creative.
Adaptable and flexible: Can change and/or go with the flow.

Collaborative and team-oriented: Works with others to accomplish tasks.

Always in training: Continually learning and adding to their repertoire of skills.

Multi-tasking: Can perform numerous things at one time.

Future-oriented: Looks toward the future and realizes the impact of what they do today.

Remember that there are always other jobs, but not other people, memories, or days. Keep your perspective—a job is replaceable, you are not! Do not confuse who you are with your role or title. Initially, your self- esteem may wane, but you can affirm yourself and your skills by thinking positively. Things usually happen for a reason. Know that a new experience is waiting for you just around the corner. As always, when you learn what you are meant to learn and follow your intuition, you will be led in the right direction.

Journal Assignment #24

What career changes have you experienced? How did you handle them? How could further develop your resiliency for future transitions?

Chapter Eighteen

Lifelong Learning

"To attain knowledge, add things every day.
To attain wisdom, remove things every day."
—Lao Tze

To Keep Earning, Keep Learning

The key to career success is your ability to become a lifelong learner—
someone who is continually updating skills and deleting irrelevant
information from their internal database. On a regular basis, you need
to upgrade your brain. A brain is a muscle, and like other muscles in
our body, if it is not exercised or used, it will vegetate. Use it or lose it.
You need to challenge yourself to continuously learn about new and
innovative ideas and concepts.

It can be said that you become what you learn about. What or
who do you want to become? What do you need to learn about in
order to do_____? The work you choose to do impacts your
process of becoming because the experiences help to form who you are.
Know what you need learn about and where to go to get the information—your success in work and in life depends on it. Don't be afraid
to branch out, learn about new ideas, gather new information, or gain
new credentials. In many ways, you become known for what you
know. Ask yourself: What do I want to be known for? What kind of
person do I want to become?

In the competitive business world, now more than ever, knowledge is power. But it is even more important to apply what you know.
It is no longer enough to just know about things, you must put your
knowledge to work. The more access you have to information, the

greater your chance to place yourself in successful positions. The marketplace will continue to change, and so must we. We will always have to learn new skills to keep ourselves marketable. With emerging technologies and other new discoveries, we will be forced to change the way we work and live in the 21st century. We will have to find ways to apply our skills to an ever-evolving marketplace. But above all else, our most important job is to serve humanity by sharing our many gifts and to do it with love and respect. Once you create your life's work, you will find that there are infinite ways to express yourself, if you only rise to the challenge. As Ralph Waldo Emerson once said, *"All life is an experiment. The more experiments you make, the better."* Keep experimenting with your life and your work!

Lifelong Career Fitness

As I said before, career development is a lifelong process. You will always be looking inside your "career closet" to see how everything is complementing your life circumstances. To maintain a healthy career, you will need to develop a lifelong career fitness program— a lifelong workout— where you stretch and bend and become flexible to your life changes and the changes in the workplace. In the past, working out meant high-impact aerobics, pushing ourselves to the brink of exhaustion. Our motto was, "no pain, no gain."

In today's world of work, keeping a fit career will become more like doing yoga, where we tune into our inner selves. In order to make smart decisions, we will have to slow down and listen to our mind, heart, and body to see if we are comfortable with our current "position." As we practice reflection, and become more inner-focused, we will learn when to bend, when to stretch, and when to change positions completely.

We will also strive for more knowledge and experiences. In the 21st century, the educated person will no longer be the person who has learned, but who is *still learning*. And that means taking risks, experimenting, and learning from both the formal and informal classroom of life.

Whole life fitness means making wise decisions, choosing the best. When you become selective in life, you make smart choices. You choose the right jobs, people, and places to live, which ultimately gives you more of what you want out of life. In order to be selective, though, you first have to know what you want. If you don't know what you want, chances are you will settle for whatever comes along. Having a sense of who you are and what you value is the first key in becoming aware of what you want. Just like compulsive shoppers, who buy for the sake of buying but never use what they purchase, they start believing that they really need them. If you can learn to buy only what you truly want and need, you would not only have more money, you'd have more space and more appreciation for those things you did buy.

Choosing a simpler lifestyle will lead to more money in your pocket which will lead to more time on your hands. Our consumer-oriented society teaches us to spend beyond our means, and then we end up having to work, instead of choosing to work. You have to learn to say "No," especially to the job that is not the right fit.

As an empowered person, you can wait for the right job to come along, feeling confident that it will. Only people who are dis-empowered and are unaware of their self-worth end up settling for second-best. But when you are selective, you get more of what you really want and less of what you don't. The wonderful news is that there is enough for everyone. But an abundant life only comes to those who actively seek it out. Again, relying on your intuition leads you down the right path. To get more of what you want out of life, you have to be self-aware, but you also must have a selection process in place. Ask yourself does this job, position, company meet my criteria? Yes, No, Maybe? If not, let it go and move on to something better. If you are not sure, you need to do more soul searching. If yes, then go for it!

Find Your Unique Life Balance

If you think of your life like an experiential pie, you will begin to see that your work is only one slice of the pie. There are many others you can taste. If you put too much emphasis on one or two pieces, other pieces lose their flavor. The recipe for keeping your career energized is to *find your unique balance* and to indulge in each delicious bite after bite!

Love
Labor
Leisure
Learning
Self Development
Relationships
Hobbies
Spirituality

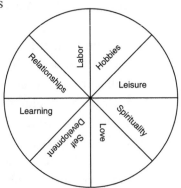

Make sure you are getting equal helpings from all of your life areas: Love, Labor, Leisure, and Learning. Look at each day as a chance for you to *share your gifts*. When you choose to work from a place of love and openness, you can perform wondrous miracles and put your distinctive mark on the world.

Smart people know that practicing balance in life is of the utmost importance to staying healthy, happy, and in a state of readiness for their life's work.

- Know when to say "enough is enough," especially regarding food, alcohol and sexual behavior.
- Know your standards and stick to them. Never settle!
- Give thanks to those people or "spirits" in your life.
- Break your routine. Drive a different route home from work. Tackle a big project. Research something new about technology.
- Learn to laugh at yourself and at life. The sooner you do this, the better you will feel.
- Learn to appreciate your uniqueness.
- Smile as often as possible. If you cannot think of anything to smile about, go to a park and watch children or dogs playing.
- Release yourself to the universe, and believe that it will take care of you. (The universe provides, it really does).
- Trust your intuition. If something deep within is speaking to you, take notice, listen to it. Your intuitive nature will guide you to your highest good.
- Take care of yourself in all ways that matter to you.
- Invest in your life. Do something positive that will have a long-term affect, i.e. start a workout program, learn about the stock market, or move to a more desirable location.
- Bring balance to your thoughts and feelings. By keeping checks

and balances on your emotions and thoughts, you can be more in control of your life, your career, and your destiny.

True life success, though, is finding your unique life balance and enjoying all that the precious gift called *life* has to offer. Ralph Waldo Emerson defined success this way:

To laugh often and love much;
To win the respect and the affection of children;
To earn the approbation of honest critics and endure the betrayal of false friends;
To appreciate beauty; To find the best in others; To give of one's self;
To leave the world a bit better, whether by a healthy child, a garden patch,
or a redeemed social condition;
To have played and laughed with enthusiasm and sung with exultation;
To know even one life has breathed easier because you lived—
This is to have succeeded.

You Have the Power to Create

As Leo Buscaglia once said, *"The life and love we create is the life and love we live."* The future is yours to create. You can use the power of your thoughts to imagine the kind of life and career that you desire, and then you can take steps to create your vision. But first, you have to believe that you have this power.

As we move further into an age of enlightenment, we will become more progressive and open in our thinking and living. We will challenge ourselves to find more enlightened ways to live and work. We will also become more intentional in how we behave. We will recognize that the more we share with others, the more we receive in kind. We will learn that we have the power to create whatever we desire simply by thinking the highest thoughts and projecting our visions onto the universe. And that collectively, we can make a positive difference in raising the consciousness level of our world. We will finally realize the power of choice—choice in our thoughts, behavior, actions, and work.

We will choose to live in enlightenment and return to holding things sacred, like family, friendship, respect, honesty, and hard work.

We will:
Continuously find ways to apply our unique gifts and talents.
Learn to tap into our intuitive nature to create a more
meaningful life.
Believe in abundance.
Create work that allows us to express who we really are.
Consider the long-term effects of our thoughts and behavior.
Practice active reflection which will help us to develop insight.
Do work that is meaningful for ourselves and others.
And know that we have the capability to create
the kind of life and work we desire.

You can choose to live your life in enlightenment. You have already initiated the process by choosing to *Get Smart!* It is now up to you to put your newly-discovered knowledge into practice, and make your dream of creating your life's work a reality.

Appendix A
Internet Career Resources

The Electronic Job-Search

The Internet has expanded the job search process by making available position announcements to the whole world. In some ways, it makes it easier because you have access to the information. On the other hand, it makes the job hunt more competitive, as more people know about available positions, more will apply.

However, no career development book would be complete without information about job searching online. Listed below is a small sampling of websites with career information and job postings. Keep in mind that there are thousands of career-related sites, so it will take some time and experimentation until you find the ones most useful to you. Note: I make no recommendation of any of these sites, I merely provide them for your information. All sites were active as of this book printing.

Sample General Websites

America's Job Bank
www.ajb.dni.us
This site is operated by the U.S. Department of Labor.

Careers.Org
www.careers.org
This site has a lot of career advice and information.

CareerPath
www.careerpath.com
This site includes want ads from selected newspapers across the nation.

Career Mosaic
www.careermosaic.com
Gives job hunting advice.

Cool Jobs
www.cooljobs.com
Off the wall job listings.

Job Hunters Bible
www.jobhuntersbible.com
This site was developed by Dick Bolles, author of the What Color is Your Parachute?

HeadHunter
www.headhunter.net
This site is for executive level job seekers.

Employment 911
www.employment911.com
This site is an on-line employment site.

Flip Dog.Com
www.flipdog.com
This site claims to have more jobs than the popular monster board.

Internet Career Connection
www.iccweb.com
Vast career resources, including articles, information, and job listings.

JobOptions
www.joboptions.com
Job listings on-line.

Job Sleuth
www.jobsleuth.com
General Job Search Site.

Job Star
www.jobstar.org
This site contains job listings as well as salary information.

JobTrak
www.jobtrak.com
This site links with colleges and universities across the nation. You may need a password to use the site. If you are an alumni of a participating university, you can probably call the Career Center and obtain it.

JOBWEB
www.jobweb.com
This site is operated by the
National Association of
Colleges and Employers and
connects students with employers.

Job Safari
www.jobsafari.com
This site lists corporate human
resource web pages.

The Monster Board
www.monster.com
This site lists jobs worldwide
and includes keyword and geo-
graphical search options.

USA Jobs
www.usajobs.opm.gov
This site is operated by the
Office of Personnel
Management and lists federal
jobs all over the United States.

Virtual Career Fairs
www.careerfair.com also
www.diversitycareerfair.com
This site is 24/7 career fair.

Sample Industry Specific Websites

Higher Education Jobs
www.chronicle.merit.edu

Accouting and Finance Jobs
www.accounting.com

EXECUNET
www.execunet.com

Future Step
www.futurestep.com

Marketing Classifieds
www.marketingjobs.com

Federal Agency Jobs
www.fedjob.com

MBA Jobs
www.mbajob.com

Computer Jobs
www.computer-jobs.net

Sales, Marketing, and
Technology Jobs
www.jobblazer.com

6Figure Jobs
www.6figurejobs.com

Teaching Jobs
www.teachersonline.com
www.k-12teachingjobs.com

Finance Jobs
www.careerbank.com

Human Resource Jobs
www.shrm.org

People Bank-Great Britain
www.peoplebank.com

Technology Jobs
www.hotjobs.com

Medical Jobs
www.medistaff.com
www.healthjobs.co.uk
www.medjobs2000.com

Security Jobs
www.securityjob.com

Public Sector Jobs
www.publicsectorjobs.com

Intelligence
www.intelligencecareers.com

Writing Jobs
www.writerwrite.com

Sample Employer Websites

Abbott Laboratories
www.abbott.com

Avis
www.avis.com

Boeing
www.boening.com/employment

CIA
www.cia.gov
Deloitte & Touche
www.us.deloitte.com

DuPont
www.dupont.com/careers

EDS
www.eds.com/career

General Electric
www.gecareers.com

Lucent Technologies
www.lucent.com

Mars, Inc
www.mars.com

Milliken & Company
www.milliken.com

Nordstrom
www.nordstrom.com

Office Depot
www.officedepot.com/jobs

Pfizer Incorporated
www.research.pfizer.com

Southern Company
www.southernco.com

Texaco
www.texaco.com

WORLDSPAN
www.worldspan.com

Sample Entrepreneurship Websites

All Business
www.allbusiness.com

BigSmart
www.smarty.bigsmart.com

Big Step
www.bigstep.com

Business Resource Center
www.morebusiness.com

Business Connections
www.businessconnections.com

Business at Home
www.gohome.com

Enterprise Online
www.enterprise.org

Entrepreneur Magazine's Small Business Square
www.entrepreneurmag.com

EntreWorld
www.entreworld.com

Fast Company
www.fastcompany.com

Freeagents (freelancers, consultants, & independent contractors)
www.freeagent.com

Foundation for Enterprise Development
www.fed.org

Guru (media, finance, IT, web development jobs)
www.guru.com

Small Business Administration
www.sbaonline.sba.gov

Minority Business Entrepreneur Magazine
www.mbemag.com

National Business Association
www.nationalbusiness.org

Onvia
www.onvia.com

Smart Biz
www.smartbiz.com

Small Biz Search
www.smallbizsearch.com

Working Solo
www.workingsolo.com

The Inc. On-line newsletter
www.inc.com

Trade Show Central
www.tscentral.com

The United States Patent and Trademark Office
www.uspto.gov

Appendix B
Life's Work Document

Name_____

_____

_____

My Purpose is_____

_____

_____

My Career Objective is_____

_____

_____

Short-term goals (1-12 months)_____

_____

_____

Mid-term goals (1-3years)_____

_____

_____

Long-term goals (5-10 years)_____

_____

_____

Academic & Career Background
Name & Location of School   **Degree or Certificate**

Dates

_____

_____

_____

_____

_____

_____

Favorite school subjects_____

Special licenses or training_____

Name & Location of Company   **Title/Duties**

Dates

_____

_____

_____

_____

_____

_____

_____

Interests & Abilities
Something I have always dreamed of doing is

_____

_____

10 things I love to do

_____   _____
_____   _____
_____   _____
_____   _____
_____   _____

Hobbies
(Avocations)_____

_____

Community Service or Volunteer Activities

_____

_____

I have a natural gift or talent for

_____

_____

I would like to learn more about

_____

_____

Personality & Skills
Words that describe me

_____

_____

My Holland Code is_____
My MBTI Type is_____

Possible Career Options for me

_____

_____

My Areas of Expertise include_____

_____

My Areas for Improvement include_____

_____

Awareness & Empowerment
I want to work
for_____doing_____

Meaningful work for me would be something where I

_____

_____

Something I will do to motivate myself is

_____

_____

Something I will do to empower myself is

_____

_____

An inspirational quote that I try to live by

_____

_____

_____

This document can be used to pull together
what you have learned about yourself while reading
Get Smart! About Modern Career Development.

Appendix C
Small Business Resources

Business Plan Outline

Cover Sheet: Business Name, Address, Phone Number, Principals

Statement of Purpose/Executive Summary

Table of Contents:

Section One: The Business
- A. Description of the business
- B. Products/Services
- C. Market Analysis and Marketing Plan
- D. Location
- E. Competition
- F. Management and Operations
- G. Personnel
- H. Application and effect of loan or investment

Section Two: Financial Data
- A. Sources and applications of funding
- B. Capital equipment list
- C. Break even analysis
- D. Projected income statements
- E. Projected cash flow statements
- F. Projected balance sheets
- G. Assumptions to financial projections
- H. Historical financials (for existing business)

Section Three: Supporting Documents
> Personal resumes, letters of reference, personal financial statements, copies of leases, diagrams of facilities, letters of intent, purchase orders, contracts, marketing brochures, or anything else relevant to the business plan.

Employment Taxes

Businesses with employees must withhold State and Federal employee taxes and pay employer taxes. Both must be deposited (monthly or quarterly) in any Federal Reserve Bank. Money withheld includes a percentage for Social Security, Medicaid taxes, Federal Unemployment Tax (FUTA). Other taxes include Self Employment Tax, Sales Tax, Property Taxes, Worker's Compensation. Check with your accountant or Small Business Development Center for specific information. Or call the Internal Revenue Service 1-800-829-1040 or the IRS Publications line: 1-800-829-3676.

For Further Reading

Boldt, Laurence G. *Zen and the Art of Making a Living: A practical Guide to Creative Career Design.* New York: Arkana, 1993.

Bolles, Richard. *What Color is Your Parachute?* Berkeley: Ten Speed Press, 1997.

Bolles, Richard. *The Three Boxes of Life.* Berkeley: Ten Speed Press, 1981.

Covey, Stephen. *The Seven Habits of Highly Effective People.* New York: Simon & Schuster, 1989.

Edwards, Paul and Sarah. *Finding Your Perfect Work: The New Career Guide to Making a Living, Creating a Life.* New York: Putnam Books, 1996.

Farr, Michael J. *The Very Quick Job Search: Get a Good Job in Less Time.* Indianapolis, JIST Works, 1996.

Fox, Matthew. *The Reinvention of Work.* New York: HarperCollins, 1995.

Kanchier, Carole. *Dare to Change Your Job and Your Life.* Indianapolis: JIST Works, 1996.

Kennedy, Joyce Lain. *Resumes for Dummies.* IDG Books Worldwide, Inc., Foster City, CA. 1996.

Hansen, Sunny. *Integrative Life Planning: Critical Tasks for Career Development and Changing Life Patterns.* San Francisco: Jossey Bass Inc, 1997.

Levinson, Jay Conrad. *Guerilla Marketing: Secrets for Making Big Profits from Your Small Business.* Houghton Miflin, 1998 (revised edition).

Paulson, Edward and Layton, Marcia. *The Complete Idiot's Guide to Starting Your Own Business.* New York: Alpha Books, 1995.

Sinetar, Marsha. *Create the Work You Love to Build the Life You Want.* St. Martin's Press, NY, 1995.

Sources For Career Information

America's Demographics. Reports trends as a result of population changes.

Occupational Outlook Handbook (OOH). Published every two years by the U.S. Department of Labor's Bureau of Labor Statistics.

Thomas Register. Lists more than 100,000 companies across the country.

Standard & Poor's Register of Corporations, Directors, and Executives. Listing of parent companies and subsidiaries.

Encyclopedia of Associations. Listing of more than 22,000 organizations across the United States.

Upstart Publishing has dozens of titles for all aspects of small business operation.

Magazines: *Fast Company, Success, Forbes, Working Woman, and Inc.*

About the Author

D   E   S   T   I   N   Y

Dare to Empower your Self and Tailor life Individually as Needed for You

—Michelle L. Casto

Michelle L. Casto is a Whole Life Coach who resides in Atlanta, Georgia. She holds a Master of Education from the University of South Carolina, a Bachelor of Science degree from Ohio University, and is a Certified Career Development and Customer Service Instructor, who has taught and counseled students at several major universities in the southeastern United States. As a writer, speaker, and trainer, she specializes in the areas of Romantic Relationships, Gender Communication, Career Development, Customer Service, and Stress Management. Michelle is an active member of the National Career Development Association and American Society for Training & Development. She is a qualified user of the MBTI personality assessment and Prepare/Enrich assessment for couples considering marriage.

When she discovered that there was not much practical, proactive advice on how to integrate the various life dimensions, she decided to write the Get Smart! LearningBook Series. The second Learningbook in the Get Smart! series is *Get Smart! About Modern Career Development.* Her purpose is to educate and empower people to make smarter personal and professional decisions through the Get Smart! LearningBooks and seminars.

Michelle is dedicated to lifelong learning and the power of human potential. In her spare time, she enjoys reading and researching on the topic of human development and traveling.

Index

Get Smart! LearningBooks & Seminars

Offers several personal growth services:

Assessment: The MBTI Personality Inventory and Prepare/Enrich for couples considering marriage.

Coaching: Experience more fulfillment in all of your life dimensions (love, labor, leisure, and learning) with the help of a personal coach.

Seminars: Get Smart! about romantic relationships, career development, stress management, and more!

If you would like information on our company, please write:

     Get Smart!

6131 S. Norcross-Tucker Rd., Suite 500 PMB#189

     Norcross, GA 30093

Call: (770) 281-4606 E-mail: info@getsmartseries.com

Visit us virtually: www.getsmartseries.com

Look for other Get Smart! LearningBooks:

Get Smart! About Modern Stress Management:
A Personal Guide to Living a Balanced Life (2002)

Get Smart! About Modern Romantic Relationships:
Your Personal Guide to Finding Right and Real Love (1999)

GET SMART! BOOK ORDER FORM

You may order additional copies of any *Get Smart! LearningBook* directly from us.

Please send me _____copies of *Get Smart! About Modern Career Development*
Please send me_____copies of *Get Smart! About Modern Romantic Relationships*
Please send me_____copies of *Get Smart! About Modern Stress Management*

Books are $15.95 each   _____
Plus $3.20 shipping and handling for 1- 2 books ordered   _____
$6.50 for 3-10 books ordered   _____
More than 10 call for actual shipping costs...
GA residents pay 6% tax   _____

Total   _____

Method of Payment
Check One:
Personal Check (phone number required)   _____
Money Order   _____
Credit Card— Circle: Visa Mastercard   _____

Card #_____Exp. Date_____

Authorized Signature_____
Send to:

Name_____

Address_____

Quantity Discounts Available!
***Make checks payable to: Get Smart!
                                   6131 S. Norcross-Tucker Rd.
                                   Suite 500 PMB #189
                                   Norcross, GA 30093
Telephone Orders: (770) 281-4606
E-Mail Orders: info@getsmartseries.com

Visit us Virtually: www.getsmartseries.com